Dear Teen Mom,

Real Stories, Tips, and Support from Other
Teen Moms Who Lived Through it, are Happy,
Healthy, and Successful in Life

by Lindsey Hoskins

DORRANCE
PUBLISHING CO
EST. 1920
PITTSBURGH, PENNSYLVANIA 15238

Dorrance Publishing Co

585 Alpha Drive

Pittsburgh, PA 15238

Visit our website at *www.dorrancebookstore.com*

ISBN: 979-8-89127-962-9

eISBN: 979-8-89127-460-0

Dear Teen Mom,

Real Stories, Tips, and Support from Other
Teen Moms Who Lived Through it, are Happy,
Healthy, and Successful in Life

To all the young mothers out there trying their best to make it in this life, to be a good mom, and to be happy: I believe in you. To my own children who came into my life and gave me courage and strength to never give up, and, most importantly, gave me the love I never felt before. Thank you, and I love you so much.

Table of Contents

Introduction

THIS BOOK IS WRITTEN FOR THE TEEN MOM WHO often feels alone, judged, hopeless, and scared. I want you to know that there are millions of others that have been through what you are going through in your life right now. There will be millions more after you. Despite what you grew up feeling or how society makes you feel, you have the potential and the ability to endure the pain, grow and learn from these experiences, and become successful and happy. You can be a good mom and create a beautiful life for yourself and your child if you decide to.

Let me be the first to congratulate you on being a mommy. No matter your age, I believe that being a mom is the most important thing we can do on this earth. With it comes laughter, heartache, sleepless nights, and a sense of worth you probably have never felt before because you feel like you matter now. Being a mother also comes with great responsibility. Someone is looking up to you now and needs you to make their life amazing.

I have noticed that even though there are almost a million teen parents every year in the world, there are not a lot of positive, uplifting resources out there for us to turn to for encouragement when things are really hard. And a lot of times, they are so very hard. I noticed in my own life that when I shared my doubt about my ability to raise a child and provide them and myself with a happy, healthy life, or the anxiety I felt, I was often met with judgment, criticism, and shame. I want you to realize that you are not alone. This is not impossible. You can do it, if you make the decision that you will not give in or give up on yourself and your baby and make a commitment to your success.

I was a teen mom myself, and I know how you feel. There are millions of teen moms in the world who know how you feel. I know what it is like to raise a child while growing up yourself and the unique hurdles that we have to overcome as teen moms. I have met many teen moms, through being a teen mom myself and through my career as a teacher where I now work in a program made for teen parents. I have come to realize that we have so many of the same struggles, thoughts, and issues that others do not always understand. We have so much in common and can learn from each other and support other teen moms because we have been there.

My hope is that this book will provide you with some support and direction that will help you navigate through this new chapter in your life, and that you know you are not alone. I hope you feel empowered to create the life for yourself that you want to live.

I have seen many teen moms have courage and strength they didn't know they had. I have seen them adapt to this new reality and create beautiful lives for themselves and their children. They are successful. They are happy. Their children have grown to be confident and healthy people, too. I have also seen teen parents completely lose themselves and give up, making horrible decisions, losing direction, themselves, and their children in the process. Some have not faced their past or their new reality and end up on drugs, in prison, and even dead, leaving their children to be raised by family members or placed in foster care to live and grow up with strangers. Their child eventually grows up to either not know them or even worse, despise them.

This book will share many real-life stories of teen moms who have been where you are right now. My hope is that ten years from now, you will be one of the uplifting stories at the end of this book that helps another teen mother get through the day and motivates them to want to achieve like you have. That you will look back on your life and the decisions you make now and are not filled with regret, but pride and joy and are truly at peace with your life.

The choice is yours, starting today.

PART I

Chapter 1

REALITY

OKAY, SO HERE WE ARE. HOW DID THIS HAPPEN and how did we get here? Well, brace yourselves. We had sex. One of the first realizations I had as a teen mom and heard about from other teen parents was that for some reason, the fact that everyone knows we had sex bothers us, embarrasses us, or makes us insecure because of the reactions we get from other people. Another reality is that some people will point this out every chance they get.

Like most people in the universe, we had sex. Premarital sex at that. Even though a huge portion of the population has done the same thing, we now feel like we have a gigantic sign on our forehead announcing it to the world, and we are condemned for it. I have learned that, in general, people can be quick to place judgment and shame on others. It seems that when they behave this way, they make themselves feel superior, and they need that validation. Even if individuals did the same things that you did, they did not end up pregnant, and they are not in your shoes now. Some will seem to condemn and judge. And we feel it. It hurts our feelings and makes us embarrassed by our situation.

Just be aware this is not unique to us as teen moms. The judgmental will judge. The self-righteous will condemn you, and when you make it in life, the haters will hate. So just own it. It doesn't go away. And don't let these people steal your joy and keep you from enjoying those beautiful little moments—the best parts about being a mom. This was a mistake I made that I regret. I don't know if it was myself being insecure or their being mean. It was probably a combination. But it was my perception, therefore it *was* my reality. I internalized this attention and took it personally. It affected my self-esteem, and it affected my kids because I was insecure and self-conscious all the time. As a result, I focused on the outside a lot instead of the inside. I worried about people who didn't help me, care about me, or pay my bills. I worried about the other people who didn't matter and were not going to approve of me no matter what I did. That energy should have gone to myself and my kids and nobody else.

In reality, we know that oftentimes there is so much more than just having sex that got us here. One thing that I found is we all have different reasons for getting pregnant at such a young age. It goes so much deeper than the exterior behavior of merely having sex. It's complicated, and a lot of people don't understand.

Some of us do not have a father figure in our lives and yearn for the love of a man. We trust in boys we shouldn't because we want to feel safe and comforted like we should feel from a father in our lives.

Others come from extremely abusive households and suffer from abuse, neglect, or some other life-shattering travesty that tears our family and ourselves apart. We so desperately seek an escape, believing that it will come from having a child. We truly think that this is the only way to get out.

Some of us were abused as children, and this abuse has manifested itself yet again in our lives through our relationships with others, and the abuse continues. We think it's normal. It's not.

Another common theme I see is that some kids are raised in households where things like sex, drugs, and worldly topics are considered tacky or rude to talk about and therefore are not discussed. Ever. When scenarios arise on the television or around us, we become uncomfortable and don't feel like it is acceptable to approach a parent with questions or to have conversations about what we were exposed to. A lot of teens growing up like this learn about these things from friends. You want to know about drugs, you can't ask your parents, so you ask your friend or your neighbor, who tells you all they know and lets you try theirs. You're curious about sex, so you listen to the boy who tells you to trust him, so you try it.

Others have this inner self-hatred, and we don't know why, but we hate ourselves to the point that we give ourselves away to men who take advantage of our vulnerability, and we never thought about protecting ourselves. Others come from what society considers a normal family unit with loving parents, money, status, and opportunity, yet end up on this path of teen parenting.

I always yearned for the love of a father, and I never had it. My mom was everything. She fought to protect us for years and did the best she could. We had an abundance of love from her. We didn't have money poor growing up, and she worked so hard to go to college, feed us, and make sure we had what we needed. She ended up working at a school as a secretary until she retired. She protected us from a lot and fought to provide for us, giving us a happy childhood. She was completely selfless when it came to her kids. But you see, even though my mother did so much right, my father did so many things wrong, and my self-esteem and self-image were severely impacted at a very young age.

In my mom's house, we did not discuss sex or drugs, and it was very uncomfortable when the topic arose. I would get life advice and information from friends and their parents, who were not embarrassed to have these discussions. I learned most things by trying it out. I had a very poor sense of who I was and an even lower self-worth. I never had attention and love from a man, and when it came, regardless of the form it came in, I thought it was great. I never considered what would happen in my life or thought about the future. I never saw potential in myself, and I had this inner hatred for myself.

Whatever brought us here happened, and we are here. We cannot change the past. If you figure out how, let me know and we'll be super rich together. Until then, try and come to terms with the past. Analyze and talk to someone you trust that has taken their life in a similar direction you want to take yours. You can also seek out professional help as well. In fact, I highly recommend it! It can be really helpful to work out our feelings and look at our childhood with someone who is trained to support us in analyzing what happened, helping us feel better, and planning out our future.

A therapist can help us learn how to take away the pain and suffering we have been through and move on with life. We can learn about our past and what brought us here. Then we can deal with those inner demons so that they don't appear later in life in unhealthy ways. Learn from your mistakes and the mistakes of others and apply these lessons to your life and grow as a person. This will not only make you a happier and healthier person, but you will be a better mom.

I have noticed in myself and others that dwelling on the circumstances that brought you here creates this self-pity and self-doubt I see in a lot of teen moms. It makes you feel like you can't get through hard times when you can. So, ultimately, holding on to yucky stuff from our past also makes it harder to move on in a healthy direction.

Think about it like reading a book. It is time to close that old chapter in your life. And guess what? If we are stuck reviewing the last chapter, what happened in the last chapter, how to change the last chapter, we cannot finish it and start writing the next, more beautiful chapter, creating the happy ending in our very own book.

Chapter 2

THINGS FEEL DIFFERENT WITH OTHERS

REGARDLESS OF WHERE IT CAME FROM, MY perception was that everyone acted so very differently to me after I got pregnant, and everyone's reactions seemed so extreme. I would say hi to a lifelong friend and get completely snubbed with a scoff or a dirty look. I would get an eyeroll or smirk from a church member or teacher quite often, and a couple of times people even turned and walked in different directions when they saw me to avoid me. If they weren't mean and hateful, I felt like they were overly nice and sympathetic, and this was embarrassing for me, too.

Teen boys were horrible. They were the worst. It was awkward when guy friends were all of a sudden deathly afraid of me, or when guys I didn't know suddenly were overly friendly and wanted to hang out. I can't tell you how many times I heard, "Damn, girl. I didn't know you were like that." It was offensive and cruel, and it hurt my feelings.

I wish I realized this many years before I did. It hurt me and it affected me a lot. For example, when I was in high school, I was in love with exercise and took a PE class that I loved. It was an exercise class where we did different work-outs every day. I loved that class, and it was probably the only class I have ever excelled at to this day. It was a needed stress reliever for me, and I relied on it. Many times, during high school, I would be so frustrated, I would throw my hair in a pony, put on my shoes, and just run. Run until I wasn't angry or hurt anymore. It helped me a lot, and I needed that class.

One of the first adults I talked to was my PE teacher. I was a star student in that class. After making a strange face, she had me sit out that day. She said I would sit out until she could talk to the administration and find out what to do with me. I was moved out of the class the next day and put in a woodshop class.

Pregnant people can and should exercise. Instead, I was moved into a classroom where I spent most days in the teacher's room alone because I couldn't be around the chemicals or machinery they were using on a daily basis. They could harm my baby and were not safe. I learned nothing. Except that things were very different now.

I remember going to a friend's house I met in college, and her mother was the nicest lady. But as soon as I came in, she started cleaning out her pantry and kept trying to send me home with all her food. I had food at that time. I was there for myself to have friends, and once again I felt like the one-man single-mom show. I was so embarrassed.

So yes, people will treat you differently. Know it's coming, be prepared, and have a plan, so, when it happens, it won't affect you like it did me. Not everyone is being mean. Sometimes people act certain ways out of ignorance or fear themselves, and it has nothing to do with us, even if it feels like it does.

Chapter 3

PEOPLE CAN BE SO MEAN

A HARSH REALITY COMING YOUR WAY I WANT YOU to be prepared for is that some people can and will be so very cruel. Know that when a certain type of person sees you struggle, they will use this as fuel to ignite their hate fires. Prepare yourself and know it is coming when you least expect it and out of nowhere.

Let me give you an example of the cruelty that comes out of nowhere. When I was a young single mother of two, I would try so very hard to take my boys to church. I remember that by the time I got dressed, got them dressed and fed, changed my clothes at least once because I had been peed on or spit up on, I would be so tired and not want to even go anymore. Nevertheless, I thought that this was what good mommies were supposed to do. So, we went.

One morning I showed up a little early, but I was so tired from a really rough morning with my little family of three. I sat in the last row behind a family I had known for years.

They were friends with my grandparents, who had both passed. I had known and trusted them for years and smiled and felt comforted when I saw them. As I was sitting with my children, this man, Mr. K I shall call him, turned around, looked at me and my boys, grinned, and then turned to his daughter.

He then said, "Hey, you know what they call people that make the same mistake twice?"

She responded, "What?"

He turned, looked back at me, and said, "Stupid!"

They both laughed, and he gave me a dirty look. They went on to sing with the congregation and be edified by the spirit of the sermon while I sat in bewilderment. I felt dumb that it took so long to realize what was happening.

After a few similar experiences like this, I quit taking my boys to church. I no longer felt that a good mommy sat through a sermon with perfectly behaved children. I started to feel that a good mommy protected her children from harm, even if that meant protection from judgment that they received at a church that could potentially hurt their self-esteem and self-worth at such a young age.

Unfortunately, church is a place where the teen mom gets judged and shamed pretty harshly, and it happens a lot. I had student who told me about the pastor cracking jokes about them on Mother's Day during the sermon in front of the entire congregation. And everyone laughed. A couple weeks ago a student of mine was so excited to return to church with her baby. When she got there, the pastor would not shake her hand or acknowledge her. Another older woman commented she had gained so much weight since she last saw her that she was unrecognizable now. She was hurt.

Church is supposed to be a welcoming place without people who behave like this, and I think that is why it has such a negative effect on us teen moms. It is so unexpected when it happens, and our guard is down because we are supposed to be safe there.

Another time my son had cavities, and I took him to the dentist. The dentist asked a list of questions, to which I replied with honesty, genuinely wanting to get my son's teeth fixed. One of the questions was about what my son ate and drank on a typical day. I had always given my son juice in a bottle. I didn't know that it was bad. In fact, I thought I was being a better mom because I would water it down, so he was drinking extra water. The dentist became angry and told my son's father and myself that we were horrible parents and that we needed to be parents and not friends to our child. I wasn't a terrible mother. I loved my son so much and would never hurt him intentionally. I really did not know. The dentist was a jerk, and instead of doing his job and educating us, he put us down and insulted us. It wasn't necessary. I guess we both didn't realize at the time that MY insurance was feeding HIS children. HE was working for ME! He had no right to disrespect me in front of my child!

Just because we don't have a cookie-cutter family that society deems as normal or acceptable does not mean my kids and I don't have worth. I didn't have to allow people to treat myself or my children poorly or like second-class citizens. And neither do you, because they are not. Looking back, I have no regrets, and I feel that I made the right choice for me and my boys. Mr. K is and always has been a sad man who needed to kick a teen mom when she was down to inflate his ego. HE was not adhering to the gospel he preached. It was his problem, not mine.

It is important that you realize that you and your child ARE a family. Your family is just as important as the wealthy family down the street with the big house and fancy cars that we don't necessarily have just yet. You deserve to be treated with respect as a mother regardless of your age, and your child deserves just as much as every other child does.

Chapter 4
PEOPLE CAN BE GENUINE

NOT EVERYONE IS HATEFUL AND MEAN. SOME people really do have good intentions and want to help you. If you need help or support, and someone offers to help, let them. Don't be ashamed to accept help when you need it. You can pay it forward when you are in a place in life to be able to do so.

Looking back, I do feel that the mother of my friend in college was really just trying to help me. When I was embarrassed, it was my issue. Not her. She was genuinely trying to help me and had compassion for me as a young single mother.

One night I was driving my car through town, and I was pulled over by a police officer because a brake light was out on the back of my car. I will never forget the look on this man's face when he asked for my registration, and I opened my glovebox, which had nothing but tampons in it. I couldn't find my driver's license, my registration was expired, and I did not have insurance. I wasn't trying to blatantly break the law. I was a hot mess, and it was apparent.

This officer gave me a ride home on the promise that I would have someone pick up the car for me and fix everything within a week. On the way back, he talked to me and didn't judge me, and it helped me so much. He could have towed my car, gave me tickets, and it would have been my fault because I should have been more responsible. Instead, he used the time to talk to me like a person and teach me.

My boss in college was another person who just accepted me, guided me, and supported me nonstop. She was overly hyper, like me, and I wanted to be like her when I became her age. I would drop off my oldest at school, my youngest at preschool, go to class, and work at the college in between classes. Some days I would show up exhausted, looking like I had been dragged to work behind my car instead of driving it there. Despite my appearance, she never said anything negative to me. She smiled, we laughed, and she gave me some great life advice daily.

One Thanksgiving she pulled me aside and gave me an envelope with cash in it. She said that every year she and her husband chose a family and sponsored their Thanksgiving meal, and she would like to cover mine. What a tremendously generous gesture! One Christmas, she gave me boxes of decorations to decorate my little apartment for my boys. I still pull those decorations out every year and smile when I think of her generosity and unconditional acceptance of me, and it reminds me to pay it forward now that I can. Another person who accepted me and supported me was my social worker at the welfare office. I had gone in twice when I found out I was pregnant and left twice in tears. They treated me terribly. They talked down to me and talked to me like I slapped a baby on the way there to ask them for help. I was treated like trash every single time I entered that building. It was a humiliating experience. Every single time. This is a common experience among us teen moms. It occurs too often and is not okay even though it happens frequently. At the time, I only knew it happened to me, and it was hard. I needed the help, so I kept going back.

The third time I went to apply for help, I met Lanny. He was my worker for years while I was in school. He was serious, didn't laugh or talk much, but was the nicest, most genuine man. I remember one day we were having some kind of regular check-in like they required everyone to do—probably to make sure I wasn't selling my food stamps on the black market for drugs or some other check in that we were required to do. We were going over the same tedious paperwork and he exhaled and closed his stack of papers and looked up at me. He sighed, looked me in the eyes, and told me that I was different than the others that came into his office. He said I didn't belong there. He said I was better than this and he wanted to see me succeed. He never judged me, and sometimes he talked to me like a grown-up and sometimes as a child in the perfect combination. He really pushed me to continue my education and work to achieve more. I am so thankful for that man and his support.

Another example of people just being kind to a young mom was when I was working toward my teaching credential. We had to take a mandatory CPR class and would receive a certification that we would have to show proof of to start our student teaching jobs. I just did not have the fifty dollars. It may as well have been 2.5 million required, because the funds were just not there. And I couldn't think of a way to get it. Legally. When I explained this to my professor in shame, she immediately pulled out her checkbook and wrote me a check and paid it. She said something like fifty bucks won't be able to stand in my way and to just to pay her when I could. She wanted to help, and I accepted it and am so thankful for her generosity.

Try and focus in, not out. What I mean is pour your energy and efforts on you and your little one and ignore the people who are just plain shitty people. Shitty people are not happy or secure in themselves, and that is their problem, not ours. Look at the good and the people who really care and want to help. You can pay it forward someday.

The reality is that people will make assumptions about you and where you came from and where you are going. Let them. I know this is a lot harder than it sounds. Trust me, as someone that has been there. Let them make assumptions. And while both of you focus on you, you will progress in life while they watch you and remain stagnant in their own life.

Ignore anything and anyone that are not supporting you in your growth or helping you succeed right now.

Another reality is that being a teen is hard. Parenting is hard. Being a teen parent seems impossible. It is not. It's hard. We are complicated and so are our lives. But the reality is also that it is possible to be successful, raise happy, healthy children, and take our lives where we want them to go, not where society tells us we are going or destined to go.

Chapter 5

THE GOOD PARTS OF BEING A TEEN MOM

WAIT, WHAT DID THAT JUST SAY? ARE THERE good parts? And this crazy woman is going to talk about it? Yep. I said it. I shall leave my address out to avoid the protesters that would come to my house and throw bricks at my windows for saying such ludicrous things, but I'm going to go there. And I'm going to stay there for a second.

There are, of course, positives and negatives of being a teen mom. Most of the time, the negatives overpower the positives and are the focus in our lives and the focus of everyone around us. But get this: there are good things. A lot of them. I promise.

I often meet older, former teen moms and I ask this question a lot: "What was the best part of being a teen mom?" These former teen moms are older now, and many of them have had more children at an older age, so I ask about their opinions on what is the difference between not being a teen mom from being a teen mom. I notice we acknowledge similar positive aspects of being a teen mom, and that we actually miss parts of being a teen mom!

The first positive thing about being a teen mom was my age. I had so much energy as a young mom. I was light-hearted and fun. I would get off work, and my son would want to go to the park. So we went. I would be on my feet all day at work, lifting heavy boxes and walking around non-stop, and still have the energy to pick up and go when I got home. We had fun. Tons of fun. We played sports, we went down the slide together, we rode bikes, we went on walks, and we enjoyed each other's company. This was a regular occurrence as a teen mom.

Now, I am almost forty and have a child that is four years old. When I get home from work and my little guy asks to go to the park, I say old-lady things like, "Hold on, let me unwind for a second. It's been a long day," and "Okay, let me start this laundry and get dinner started really quick," which usually turns into, "Wait, let's eat first and do homework," and is typically followed up with, "Mommy is tired now. Let's snuggle and read a book or watch TV tonight instead."

As a teen mom, I was full of energy and could easily keep up with a toddler. I also enjoyed these outings just as much as my son, and it was such good quality time for us. I would take him on a bike ride across town, stop and eat a sack lunch, or have a picnic lunch, and head home. A couple of times I didn't have a ride to check in with my homeschool teacher, so I just put him on the bike, and we rode there. I would take my son to the gym, and he would play in the play zone with other children, and we would follow up with a mommy-and-son swim session. If I attempted that now, I would probably follow up with a 911 call requesting an ambulance and some oxygen and medical attention. It makes me tired thinking about it! It just is not that effortless for me anymore.

Another positive thing about being a teen mom was that, again, because of my age, I felt like I could relax and let loose and enjoy our quality time, and we had fun. Lots of it. At times, I could be spontaneous and fun, and I didn't worry or stress over little things like I do now.

Let me give you an example. One time I was watching my best friend's son, and both of our boys had a box of cereal. One threw a piece and the other retaliated. Before long, we had a full-blown food fight. They had a blast. So did I, and we destroyed my living room in the process. I just let loose, had fun, and didn't worry about the mess until afterward. It didn't bother me one bit.

That would never happen in my house now. Absolutely not! I would stress about the mess, the chaos would annoy me, and as an adult, I know that name-brand cereal is expensive and would not want to waste the money.

When I reflect on my parenting as a teen, this was a great quality. It was good for my son, good for me, and didn't harm anything but the carpet.

As a young person, I talked a lot. Probably too much. Most young people do. This was incorporated into my parenting style and in my relationship with my boys. We talked. A lot. About everything. A lot of kids cannot come to their parents with certain things. I can honestly say that I have a really open relationship with my kids, and we discuss everything in our lives. When my son was in middle school, he stayed home one day, and I got a frantic call from the vice principal of the school. Someone had put on a bear costume and ran through the PE class hosted at the park and disrupted it. He thought maybe it was my son. But you see, my son and I were close. I knew of the incident before the VP called. It was another child who called my son to relay the prank and brag about the chaos he caused. I told the vice principal that I was with my son, I knew about the incident, and that he was accusing the wrong child. I had a good relationship with the administrators at the school, so they believed me. He proceeded to ask me to tell him who it was. My response was that it was not my son, and nobody was hurt, so he would have to figure it out on his own.

Looking back, I am so happy with the choice I made as a parent to talk to my children because I know I created a safe environment for them to talk to me about the very real things kids are facing now. On many occasions, their friends would come to my house when they needed to talk about something, too. I was real. I was relatable and open about the good, the bad, and the ugly in my life. And because of my age, I was relevant when I spoke to them. We talked so much. Because of this, my boys were stronger than I was when they were faced with certain situations because we had talked about these scenarios before, during, and after they occurred.

Another positive is that some people are going to leave your life. Yes, you are reading that right. I know this is hard to accept, but some of those people needed to go anyway. One time, a student came in and cried. She felt so alone. She had so many friends and now could only think of one she still had. I talked with her and told her about my story, and how it really is a good thing in the end, even though it totally sucks while it happens. We talked, and she worked and went home.

As I was sitting at home scrolling through the news stories on my phone, a story popped up on my phone. It was a woman I went to school with. She was horrible to me. After my son was born, I went out for a night. I went up to her and her friends to say hi, and she basically asked what I wanted and why I was there. She was like, "Don't you have friends over there or something?" Again, she humiliated me, and it was fun for her to do it. Well, in this news story, she had been arrested for stealing thousands of dollars in chlorine to make drugs from a store in our town. Her mugshot popped up, and pictures of her stealing in the store were posted all over the internet. She is currently in hiding, according to the story, as she has a warrant out for her arrest.

I couldn't wait, I called my student. I told her another story about one of the "mean girls." I asked her to trust me and let karma take its course. It is not always a bad thing to lose people. To focus on herself right now.

These people who are so hateful to us are not happy people. I am happy, and I don't treat people like that. The problem is not you; it is them. They are dealing with their own severe problems that will manifest later in their life. They are doing you a favor by leaving your life. Trust me!

My son literally saved my life. When I had my son, my relationships with most of my friends changed. I told one of my friends I was pregnant, and her response was, "Well, you ain't kicking it with us no more." My other friends didn't say those exact words, but it was different now with them, too. It hurt at the time, but let me tell you, what a blessing!

I am still friends on social media with this girl, and her mentality and life seem to be in the same place it was when we were in high school together. She posts half-naked selfies of her smoking weed and drinking like all day, every day. She never went to school, and her grammar and spelling are horrific. She never grew up. But I did. I had to, and I am so very thankful my son was the catalyst for the separation between myself and these people I called my friends. I didn't want them around him when he was a baby. It wasn't safe. They fought for fun. They did cocaine when they wanted to lose weight. They partied all of the time. And because I protected him from them, I was also protected, and I didn't even realize it.

Let me give an example. After my son was born, I was in a friend's wedding. I got dressed and went, leaving my son with my mom. I was nursing, so I leaked breastmilk all over my dress and had to leave soon after the ceremony. It was so embarrassing. But let me tell you this. At the after-party of this wedding, there was a fight. A bad one. My other friend's mom and dad were both shot. Her mom lived, her dad did not. I was not there because I had to go back to my son. It seemed like an inconvenience at the time, but it spared me from being there when it happened. There have been many experiences like this where I, needing to go home and be a mom, spared me from a lot of traumatic experiences. Again, what a blessing.

Finally, you have someone who looks up to you and loves you like you have never been loved before. An unconditional love you only get from having a child. And this is pure joy. Someone on this earth thinks that you are perfect. Sure, they're babies and will grow up to know we have faults. They will turn into teens and be mad at us seventy-five percent of the time. But for right now, ENJOY that in this moment; you are the most important person on Earth to this child. Right now, you are perfect, and you are enough. You matter. Remember this when you feel low, and when it's really hard, and when you feel like you can't take much anymore. Take this responsibility seriously and enjoy the beautiful moments of being a mommy.

Chapter 6

KNOW YOUR OPTIONS

OUR REALITY AND OUR ENTIRE LIVES ARE CHANGING fast. What do we do now? How can we even imagine ourselves in a happy, financially stable place in our lives, considering where we are now and how far we need to go to get to where we want to be? Believe it or not, you do have options. You have a choice. If you make the decision to continue the pregnancy, have and raise your baby, you have options. Yes, even though you are still a teenager, you are now raising a child and you have a say in what happens next. You *can* get your education, have a career, make goals, and achieve those goals. You *can* be very successful in life if you want to.

Where do we start? First, seek out and familiarize yourself with different resources and educational paths and find out what is out there and available to help you. Know and learn your options and use your voice to communicate to others around you about what your needs and expectations are. Communicate what path you want to take to finish school and why it works best for you. If you make a choice, and it is not working, you can also choose to change how you are going to move forward.

You will get opinions and advice galore, so be prepared. I have found that the wrong people give advice to anyone who will listen, and so many people take random advice from the wrong person for some reason. The man missing teeth tells you what dentist to see, the abused housewife gives relationship advice, and the mother with terribly behaved children will tell you how to discipline your child. Listen to advice objectively and consider the source. Just because it comes from someone you like does not mean it is good advice. On the contrary, it may not be horrible advice just because it comes from a person you don't really enjoy.

Don't let others influence your final decisions in life if you don't want to. You can decide what you need and what you want right now. Look at the person giving you advice. Do they know what they are talking about? Are they the example you want to follow? You wouldn't go to your hairstylist to give you advice on what material to use on a tooth filling or the dentist to ask for a diet and exercise plan for weight loss. Go to the experts, people who have knowledge, education, and experience regarding what you need help with. Ask your doctor, your teachers, people that have experienced what you are having questions about and have had positive outcomes.

Not everyone has your best interest at heart, and those who do may not have the best answer or know what you need in your unique journey. So, you get to decide to take the advice or simply leave it where it was given and not take it. You are the one who will wake up tomorrow and deal with the advice you took and the decisions you made today.

FINISHING HIGH SCHOOL

One of the first major decisions you will be faced with as a teen mom will be how you are going to finish your high school education. You will have different pathways available to do this and will need to pick the one that best suits your unique situation.

For example, do you want to physically go to school with the same peers as before you were a parent? Do you need to go to work now that you have these new responsibilities? Are you able to stay home with your child, and are you capable of doing work on your own? If so, is your home a safe environment where you can accomplish this?

Everyone is different, and you will have different family dynamics, needs, and goals than other people. You should consider all of this when making your decision. What worked for me may not work for you. What works for you may not work for others, and that is why there are different options to choose from.

TRADITIONAL SCHOOLS OFFER PARENTING CLASSES

There are several school districts that offer classes that are created just for teen moms. When I was in school, there were classes that took in the children of teen moms. You could go to school during the day, and one of the class periods was spent in the classroom where your child was. In these classes, you learn about parenting and receive a lot of support and resources.

My best friend in life was also a teen mother. She utilized this resource and loved it. She got to spend time with her baby as well as time with her friends on campus. Her home life was not the healthiest, so it was good for her to physically be out of there during the day. She liked the teachers, and they helped her a lot. They supported her and taught her how to be a mom while connecting her to useful resources that helped her a lot. She loved that she could have a perfect balance of time with her friends at traditional school, remain physically close to her baby, and spend time with him during the day. She needed this in order to successfully earn her high school diploma.

DAYCARE OR PRESCHOOL

Another option is to take your child to a home daycare or a preschool if they are old enough and to go to school or go on a home study program and work. There are programs to help you pay for this childcare so that you can continue your education and work if you need to. This is a good option, too, because it is good to be on a schedule and to have your child used to a routine that they will continue throughout their life. Some parents need this rigid schedule to be successful.

Remember that you do not have to rely on a family member or someone you know to watch your child. Just because you are related to someone does not mean they are necessarily the type of person you want to be around your child eight hours a day. You can still love your family and have those healthy boundaries. You are paying someone to care for your baby, or the welfare office is paying someone on your behalf. Regardless of the source, they are being paid and are required to follow the expectations that you have as a mother. If that does not happen, you have the right to move your child to another place for care. I have seen this a few times and experienced it myself.

For example, a former student of mine was struggling with these boundaries on her journey. Her mother was watching her child while she attended school and was an amazing grandmother who sincerely loved her granddaughter with all her heart. She was not a mom and did not have to be. She loved her role as the doting grandmother, and her granddaughter loved being with "Nana." How lucky was my student to have a free babysitter that she knew her daughter was safe with, right?

Well, "Nana" did not say no, did not discipline, nor did she make healthy meals. They played every day, all day. The little girl got whatever she wanted from Nana. Well, here was the problem. This is wonderful for weekend visits with Nana, but eight hours a day, every day, was not necessarily best for the teen mom or her daughter.

My student came home from work and school every day and had a responsibility to feed her daughter healthy food. To bathe her. To teach her right from wrong, and to not just laugh when the little girl threw her soup from the table, making a silly, cute face. She needed to discipline her so that it did not happen again, because she did not grow up to be a disrespectful child that nobody but her Nana liked. It strained the relationship between my student and her mom because my student was frustrated with what would typically be great short-term help. This student applied for a program that would help her with childcare and enrolled her child in a facility that respected her boundaries as a mother. This made a huge difference in the stress level of my student and lessened some of the tension she was feeling with her mother.

A teen mom I worked with years ago would leave her baby with a friend of hers while she worked part time, because her friend didn't work and loved her baby. Well, the friend also loved to smoke weed. It was never a problem, and they did it together before she had her daughter. The friend was getting high while watching her daughter and assumed, because they both loved it, it was okay.

Well, my friend picked up her daughter and drove home one day to find the end of a blunt in her daughter's diaper when she changed her. Her daughter either ate it and passed it, or grabbed it and it fell in her diaper. My friend was pissed. She felt betrayed, and this incident ultimately ended their friendship. Her friend was caught off guard and could not understand why she was so upset. She never hid that she smoked and assumed it was okay, and the weed in the diaper was a simple mistake. Nobody died—what was the big deal? She was a great friend, and loved the little girl, but she should not have been given the responsibility to care for her, as she was still an irresponsible teen herself. Had these clear boundaries been set, these two may have maintained their friendship and could have avoided the situation where her daughter was clearly not in the best care.

Another friend of mine growing up had siblings, and her mother at home in the evenings. She would drop her son off every evening when she went to her waitressing job. They babysat her son nearly every night. Nobody was paid; it was forced upon her siblings, and they did it because she did not give them a choice. There was not one person in charge, but rather, her son ran in and was at home away from home. He watched TV, and basically did whatever he wanted. Her siblings were in charge but kind of passed responsibility to each other and were not really nice to her son. It was like he was an annoyance or a burden on the family.

It was pretty obvious to me that he was kept alive, and that was it. Not taught ABCs or 123s or fed well or loved or even liked very much. His mom probably did not know about the programs available—I know I didn't—or she felt it was easier to leave him with her brothers and sisters. Her son grew up okay, and fortunately nothing horrible happened as a result of nobody in the home being CPR certified or qualified to care for her child.

We will discuss boundaries in more depth later, but for now, let it suffice to say, you are the mom, and it is okay to have expectations of the people caring for your child. Even if they are family. It is also okay to move your child to a different childcare if you are not happy with the quality of care that your child receives.

QUIT SCHOOL AND GO TO WORK

Another option is to drop out of school and go to work full-time. To jump straight into adulthood. I see this choice made over and over again. I urge you with all of my heart not to follow this path, and to stay in school and finish, but the choice is yours. I will tell you why I highly discourage the option of quitting school.

First, without a high school diploma, you will probably make minimum wage or barely above for the rest of your life. When you get a small raise, chances are that the following year the economy will change, and minimum wage will rise to roughly what you make, bringing you to minimum wage again. Secondly, the less education and training you have, the more easily replaceable you are. At any moment, there are many people out there who will pick up your job and take it over if your boss decides they want to give it to them.

When I was working two retail jobs at the outlet mall in our town and going to school, I worked my butt off. I liked my bosses and liked the job. It was fun. People are crazy, and I was entertained quite a bit by the random experiences of working retail. But the hours were awful. Nights, weekends, and every holiday, I was at work. One Black Friday, I worked a full twenty-four hours between the two jobs. It was rough.

I remember one time calling in sick because I had a sick baby at home, and I needed to stay home to take care of him. I came to work after he was well and noticed that my hours were cut almost in half. Staying home and taking care of my son deemed me unreliable to a big corporation, and they needed to rely on someone else. Jobs that require no skill or education can do this to you. And they will. They don't account for family and outside responsibilities you have now.

One of my students came into school one day frustrated for the same reason. She called in six hours before her shift at a fast-food location and was told that she was to find coverage for her shift if she was not able to make it. This is a common practice in minimum-wage jobs. So, she spent two hours calling fellow employees, begging for help, but nobody was willing or able to come in and cover her shift. She did not find coverage, and her hours were cut to only four hours the following week.

When I got my first teaching job, my son got really sick, and I needed to stay home. I contacted my principal and apologized profusely for missing a day of work. I had anxiety about even calling in because of the repercussions of my previous jobs before completing my education. Get this. You know what this man, my new boss, told me? He said, "No problem, Hoskins. Don't worry at all about work right now. Stay home and take as much time as you need to take care of your family. I will take care of your class, so don't worry about it at all."

He also told me that he hoped my son felt better soon and checked on me the next morning to see how I was holding up. My jaw dropped. I had never heard of such a thing. I had to take a second to comprehend what he said.

For the first time in my life, I was not being punished for taking care of the most important thing in my life. My family. My pay wasn't cut, my hours were the same, and I was welcomed back with smiles and concern for my child upon my return. This is one of the first times in my life that I was so very grateful I persevered in getting my education and chasing my career. I was valued as a professional and respected, and it was okay that my son came first. What a feeling!

HOME STUDY PROGRAMS

The option that worked for me as a teen mommy was home-schooling. I was fortunate enough that my mother allowed me to live in her house and stay home with my child. With this option, I was able to do my schoolwork at home while being a mom to my son. I was required to physically come in one time per week to drop off and pick up work. I worked nights, and my family helped me with childcare so that I could go to work and earn some income. For this option, consider your home environment.

For me, this was a perfect option because my home was safe, and I was supported and was allowed to stay home and continue school and care for my child. I have known many teen moms who could not choose this option because their homes were unsafe and volatile or because their homes were so chaotic that they needed to physically be away during the day while they could. Others had parents that would not allow this option. They felt that they needed to be out of the house during the day, and so it was required of them to leave the house daily.

I currently teach at a school with a wonderful program offered to teen parents in which they can bring their babies to school with them. Students are supported in finishing high school, finding a career path, and are able to care for their babies at the same time in a safe and supportive environment. They are able to participate in support groups, meet other teen parents and even take parenting classes to earn elective credits. Try and find schools like this that genuinely care about their students like the school I work at. Schools like this are great at going above and beyond to help their students with unique needs to become successful and are also great at making connections with resources that can offer support. They also tend to hire adults who care and want to help or have lived through some tough times and really understand their students, and they can really help you!

CHOOSE WHAT WORKS FOR YOU AND YOUR BABY

There are many programs available for teen moms. Use them. I did, and they helped me feed my children, pay for childcare and clothes until I could do it on my own. That is why they are created and why they exist. To help people like us so that we can continue our education, work, and eventually be self-sufficient.

Go to the welfare office and ask for assistance. And if they send you away and treat you poorly, go back. This is common. I don't know why, but it is. It was embarrassing, but I kept going back and eventually, I found someone willing to help on my third time asking. It's unfortunate that the first two people I talked to could have helped me and instead kicked me when I was down. But you know what? Looking back, I cannot even remember either one of their names or faces because they don't matter. Keep going. Speak to a supervisor. Take someone with you so you don't feel alone. Get the help you need. Once you get approved, they will also connect you with programs to supply you with food and supplies to help you take care of yourself and your child.

Know you have options, and that you are not destined to be on welfare for the rest of your life and struggle forever. Keep in mind that it is temporary, and work hard and keep that mindset. Use the programs designed to help you finish high school and find a career path that you want for your life. I cannot stress to you enough the value of seeking out and securing help to finish school and find a career. Not a job, but a career. Imagine how it will feel to be able to buy your own food for your own house and the satisfaction you will have when you don't have to borrow money to pay the electric bill. I have experienced both life before and after and I promise you that life is so much better when you finish and chase your dreams!

Chapter 7

RELATIONSHIPS AND BOUNDARIES

RELATIONSHIPS AND BOUNDARIES ARE THINGS many teen moms struggle with. I personally have struggled with both of these my entire life, and I have to work on both areas all of the time. I have noticed that as teen parents, we tend to view and treat boundaries and relationships completely backwards. We don't speak up, we are too nice, and we don't protect ourselves in situations that we should or protect ourselves from toxic people. If we see someone else treated poorly, we get offended and stand up and defend them swiftly. However, we very rarely stick up for and protect ourselves.

Before you focus on seeking out, building, or even ending relationships with anyone, I strongly suggest that you examine your boundaries. What is a boundary and why is it so important? Well, a boundary is a line we draw between things that we allow and things that we will not allow. You need boundaries with every relationship you have. You should have boundaries with your child's father, your friends, and even your family. Boundaries are so very important because they protect us, our self-worth, our mental health, and our overall well-being. When you create boundaries, you will decide what is okay and what is not. What will you require, or how do you want to be treated? What will you absolutely not allow? Make a list of personal boundaries you think are important and that you want in your life and write down what they are. Then write down why they are important.

For example, maybe a boundary you want in your life is you will require honesty in a relationship that you are in. Maybe you want this so you are secure in your relationship and don't have to question the loyalty of the relationship and feel hurt all the time. Learn how to set those boundaries. Start small, but please start! Apply what you decide is important to your life and in your relationships. Protect yourself even better than you would protect anyone else. We should have been doing this our whole lives, but so many of us have not ever had boundaries. Everyone needs boundaries, especially the teen mom!

Know that you make the call with what is best for you and your baby. Know that because of your age, people will push boundaries a little more than they would an older mom. Stand firm and use your voice. If people want to be a part of your life, they need to support you and your choices as a mother. It may be a little uncomfortable at first, but they will learn to respect your boundaries and deal, or they won't be blessed with your presence. Period.

Any new mom sets boundaries for herself and for her child. You will also need to do this as a teen mom. When I had my son, I had so many visitors. I remember the nurses telling me that they had never seen so many visitors in a single room. I remember feeling exhausted, but my friends, family, my son's dad's family, and friends all wanted to take pictures of my baby and came by to say hi. I should have said no. I was not even close to most of these people. I didn't owe them anything. I was in labor for over forty-eight hours, followed by a cesarian section, and I should have said, "I'm tired and want to spend time with my newborn." I didn't. I didn't have boundaries, and I considered what my friends wanted when I was in the hospital having MY baby before I considered my own needs. I would never allow that now, but I just did not know how to say no, and I didn't know that it was important to say no.

One of my former students is so amazing at protecting herself and she amazes me with her strength and her strong boundaries she has made with her in-laws and her boyfriend. They were mean when she was pregnant. They brought other girls to the house and tried to set their son up with them and have him leave my student. They would talk down to her and talk badly about her. He would not stick up for her and allowed it. She drew the line. She no longer allowed them in her home and said that she would not accept this treatment from them. She didn't yell or fight or even engage. She just backed away and separated herself from them. And let them know that they would treat her with respect, or they would not be in her life. Period.

Her daughter turned one last month, and his family contacted her and apologized for the way that they treated her. They told her what a great mom she was, and they wanted to be present in the baby's life and were working on fixing the mistakes they made toward her. I was so proud of her. If she didn't stick up for herself, nobody else would have. It took courage, but it needed to be done, and the family realized that their behavior would not be accepted or tolerated. And because she was firm with her boundaries, their behavior stopped.

When looking at your relationship, please know this: You are not stuck in a relationship if you are not treated well, are unhappy, or just plain don't want to be. One lesson that my mom taught me by example was that you can get through life and don't need to rely on anyone, especially not a man if he is not good to you. As a matter of fact, if he is not great to you, you should probably think twice. I am so very grateful that my mom instilled this in me and set this example for us. She taught me that if I work hard and become independent, I can choose to be in a relationship because I want to be in it. Not because I have to.

Time and time again I see women in horrible relationships, and they don't leave. They are afraid of being alone or they cannot afford to support themselves and their children, so they stay and get cheated on or treated like crap. Not all relationships make it to forever. As a matter of fact, most do not. Some make it, that's cool. Some will not. And guess what? That is okay, too.

A common theme I see with teen moms is staying with the father of their child because they feel guilty about breaking up the family if they leave. That their child won't have a father because they ended the relationship. This was one of the reasons I stayed. It was one of the biggest mistakes I have ever made in my entire life.

One of my former students is dealing with this right now, too. She is pregnant, and her boyfriend is constantly seeking out and meeting up with other girls. She never defends herself and makes excuses over and over for him. She will say it was because he never had a dad to teach him. Another time she said, well, he was offended that she was friends with a guy on Facebook and so he was getting her back.

I myself was abused, cheated on, and he was using drugs. But I didn't want to break up my family. My thinking was so backwards and wrong. I should have felt guilty about having my son around this, and not protecting him from the severely unhealthy environment we were living in. I was allowing it by not making and enforcing boundaries!

If your relationship is not what you want, completely unhealthy, abusive, or not going in the direction you see yourself going, you have the right to walk away. You don't owe anyone any explanations if you don't want to give one. My mistake was that I was staying in a horrible and toxic relationship for all of the wrong reasons. I stayed for love, then stayed for loyalty to my kids and to have the appearance of a family for everyone else. It was a huge mistake. I wish I realized that my son and I were a complete family. We were not a stereotypical family that you see on TV, but we were enough, and I should have left way before I did. I should have realized that we were not like everyone else and that was okay. It was actually pretty cool. I wish I realized then that keeping up with the Joneses is not writing your own story—it is copying someone else's…

A lot of teen moms stay because they are bullied by their baby's father's family and terrified of going to court. I see this all the time. Let me explain. I had a student who was an amazing mother. She worked part time at a school and was working towards finishing her high school diploma. She would call me crying all the time when her child's father would get annoyed with her, call her a "dumbass" in Spanish, and embarrass her. Sometimes he would get mad at her and leave her stranded wherever they happened to be at the time. One time, he left her over an hour away from home at a mall with no way to get home. He had two cars; she had none and was using his. She would have to ask her daughter's father, this little boy who paid no child support, to borrow his car to take her daughter to school, or even to the store to purchase groceries to feed him and his daughter. His parents had a little bit of money, and he would remind her regularly that if she left, he was planning on taking her to court and taking their daughter away from her. I had to remind her multiple times that no judge on earth would take her daughter away and give her to this man because he could afford a Nissan Sentra miraculously with no job, and that she was the only one that was impressed with this. She was a great mother. Her daughter was clean and well behaved. They were bullying her and using a mother's worst fear of losing her child to keep her controlled. I see this time and time again, and it is abuse.

Another important form of boundary is to stop saying sorry for doing what you are supposed to be doing. Let me explain… Something I experience frequently is getting a frantic call from a teen mom student, and they are so apologetic and say something like, "Ms. Hoskins, I am so sorry. My daughter has a fever. We just got to the emergency room. I don't know what is wrong, and I won't be able to come in today." My answer is always the same. Don't apologize for being a mom and putting your family first. That is what you are supposed to do, and it means you are doing a good job. Remember that your child is just as important as everyone else's. When I missed a birthday party or an event, I always apologized profusely, and people were mad anyway. I always felt like I had to apologize, and looking back, I should not have. I was putting my kids first. Others should think twice before expecting otherwise from any mother!

Chapter 8
PARENTING

PARENTING IS A WILD RIDE IN GENERAL. ADD being a teenager to being a new mom and raising a human, and it's like a life roller coaster. Sometimes I felt like I was on the most beautiful ride I have ever stepped on. Comparable to a theme park family ride, with singing birds in the background, beautiful scenery, and a total sense of relaxation. Other times, I felt like I was on a ride at the county fair that was put together the night before by very questionable people. I wasn't sure that all the screws were on the ride. I wasn't sure I would make it off alive, and I wanted off.

There are so many things that I learned the hard way and so many things that I obsessed about that were so unimportant and I wasted time worrying about them. As situations and life demands arise, ask yourself, is this really important? Will it matter in twenty years when I look back on my life?

All new parents receive an abundance of advice. It can be overwhelming and confusing. Sometimes I felt like I was wearing a sign that read, "Bore me with your life story that I don't care about. Insult me by telling me what I already know or assume I don't know anything at all. Just tell me, tell me, tell me!" Do your research, read up, and ask people you observe that have qualities in their parenting that you like and look up to. Make your own decisions based on what you learn from this research. Don't just follow.

The book that was a lifesaver for me when I was a teen mom was *What to Expect When You're Expecting* by Heidi Murkoff. This was my bible during pregnancy. I read it every single day. I learned so much about what was happening in my body and where my baby was in the specific stage of development he was in. It also gave detailed descriptions of the nasty stuff that happens that no one talks about and spared me an embarrassing urgent care visit on a couple of occasions. It tells you what to look for and how to plan. It was a terrific resource for me. I highly recommend getting a book like this or finding a resource like it that suits you and will help you understand in depth what you are feeling and what is happening to you and your baby. I gladly took advice from this book, and highly recommend it.

When my son was a toddler, he said a bad word. We were staying with a family from our church at the time. They were a loving family. She was a stay-at-home mom, and he was a doctor. She volunteered, helped the less fortunate, and even made time to cook dinner for her family every night. Frankly, they were wonderful people, and I looked up to her. When my son said this word, she scoffed in disgust and suggested that I try a strategy that she practiced with her own children. She advised me to put pepper on his tongue and have him vow that he would never cuss again. I did not like the idea, but I thought she was just perfect and so I would give it a try. My mom would wash my mouth out with soap when I cussed so it made sense, and I tried it. My son screamed in agony. It got in his eyes, and it was a total disaster. I don't think that he learned anything. I sure did.

Thinking about this experience and looking at my life now, I notice that I curse like an inmate, and I am only behaving right now because I'm writing a book for teen parents. Even after eating gallons of soap as a child, I still curse like a sailor. It didn't even bother me that my son said the word. It still doesn't. It bothered others, and so I followed their advice, their standards, and their parenting styles that did not work for me. I have never done it again. It bothered me more that I physically hurt my son, and he didn't even learn anything from it. He could have learned if we had a simple conversation about it. I never did it again.

And get this: my son didn't end up being some crazed serial killer or drug-addicted monster because I didn't follow someone else's parenting style that worked in their home but I didn't want in mine. You have the choice to take other people's advice, try it, or leave it where they left it. You don't have to explain it to anyone and that is okay.

One of the most profound things I learned as a parent is this: parents make mistakes. Like, a lot of them. And get this. That does not mean you suck at being a parent and are a terrible one at that. It doesn't necessarily mean that Child Welfare Service is going to swoop in and take your child from you and give them away to another cookie-cutter family. It means that you are human. Learn from mistakes and grow as a mother. My kids and I laugh all the time about stupid parenting choices I made. So does every other family. We are all learning as we go, because mistakes happen!

The teen mom gets wild looks at the grocery store, and people are so comfortable making comments while we struggle to get through the moment that we are in. I don't miss that at all. I remember taking my son to the grocery store. He was sitting in the shopping cart, and we were walking in the store and just talking. We were having a conversation, and he was questioning me when he was learning to talk about everything, like most kids do. I was explaining something to him, something I have always done with my boys, and we were enjoying the conversation. During this talk, a man walked up and abruptly interrupted me and said, "He's not listening to you. He doesn't respect you! Look at him!"

He continued to spurt insults at me and my son and was so rude and hateful that I was humiliated and didn't know what to do. I turned around and left the store in tears. Sometimes I would spend money I didn't have to keep him quiet and spare myself the embarrassment of a dramatic exit from another store in front of a bunch of glaring strangers. So, my son got candy and learned to do it every time. I didn't realize it at the time, but I was reinforcing the tantrum behaviors by giving in and taught him that this is how you get what you want.

Looking back, if I dealt with a couple tantrums head on, it would have likely stopped. But I didn't because I was consumed with what others were thinking and what they thought of me and my family.

I am now thirty-nine years old and have a four-year-old son. Let me tell you about our trip to the store a while back. We needed to go to get a birthday present and were in a hurry. I informed him before we parked that we were getting a gift for someone else and would not be buying him a toy or anything on this trip. He responded with, "But Mom, I really want a toy." The conversation escalated, and I felt the tantrum coming on, but I was in the zone and needed the gift.

By the time we got to the aisle where the gift was located, I was carrying what appeared to be a wild animal almost completely upside down, kicking and screaming on our way to pay. He's screaming, I'm sweating and letting him know that he is on his way to the longest timeout in the history of timeouts, and guess what. No one said a word. I don't know if they noticed, but I didn't care. I was concerned with myself and my family and not what others thought of me.

I wish I had learned this earlier on. That strangers don't matter. I matter and my kids matter. You matter and your child matters. You will never please everyone, so focus on pleasing yourself.

A few days later, we were driving through an automatic car wash. I was playing games on my phone and my little guy was eating a snack. All of a sudden, he started screaming. I turned around to find that I had forgotten to roll the back window up and my son was getting wet. I frantically rolled up the window, but the damage was done. He was wet, and he was pissed. I dropped him off with his father and explained to him that ugh, yeah, he had two showers today. These things don't make me a bad mom. They make me human. The moral of the story is that it happens. To everyone. We laughed our butts off and lived and moved on.

One thing I learned, not just as a teen mom, but as a mom and through seeing many types of parents through my career, is that there are so many different parenting styles and parents show love in different ways. It is okay to be a different type of parent because that is the type of parent that you want to be.

Chapter 9
CO-PARENTING

IF YOUR RELATIONSHIP WITH YOUR CHILD'S FATHER does not make it, you will have to co-parent. What does that mean? Co-parenting means you are working together to raise your child as a team. You do this when you are not married nor dating any longer. It is hands down one of the hardest things I have ever experienced in my entire life. I have learned so much, but it has been a struggle, that is for sure. It sucks, to be honest, and I am still learning as I go. But it is so very important to do it right for your little one.

A great piece of advice my mom gave me when I had my son was to never talk badly about his dad in front of my son. She said that my son was smart enough to figure us both out, and he would on his own, but that if I said negative things about his dad to him, he would resent me for it. She was so very right.

When I was a teen mom, co-parenting was so very ugly. We battled it out in court, were completely mean and hateful to each other in front of the kids, and I personally was treated like crap. Then when he met his wife, it seemed to get even worse. They would say horrible things about me, and it would get repeated to me. They would call me names in the front yard while I dropped off my kids. I mean, it was horrible. They even requested separate parent conferences from my son's teachers, saying they could not sit through a conference with me. I was humiliated over and over by him. I was so angry and pissed that it got the best of me quite often. It is unfortunate, because we spent time and energy fighting each other that should have been focused on our children. It took years for us to figure it out. My son is twenty-three now, and years later, I have come to really like his stepmom. When we focus on our kids and not each other, we get along because we have a common goal. When you decide that you are going to work together for your kids, the other conflicts seem to work themselves out. Recently, my sons' stepbrother was tragically killed. It was a horrific murder, and my kids were devastated. It was a really hard time for our families. Looking back, I am so thankful that over the years, we have worked on our relationship, and because there was no drama between us, I was able to be there for my kids as well as their dad and stepmom. I was present for the candlelight vigil, the viewing, the reception, and the funeral. Their stepmom and I frequently text each other and check on each other. It is the opposite of what it used to be, and I can honestly say that I genuinely like and care about

her now. We have apologized for our parts in our past disagreements and expressed our desires to work together moving forward. I wish I knew then how great it could actually
be when it is done right. We could have skipped years of
drama and heartache!

Typically, I would never share this part of my struggle,
as I feel vulnerable and don't ever allow myself to be such.
This is another characteristic of the former teen moms. We
don't show weakness or allow others to see our struggles.
But I share it because almost every teen parent I have met
has had these same difficulties, and it is hard every single
time. I am telling you, it is so hard, brace yourselves. But
again, it is so necessary and worth it to do it right!

Chapter 10

SELF-CARE

You know how you take care of your baby and work super hard to do a good job? Did you know that you should be caring for yourself just as much, if not more? Always remember that you are important, too. You are special and unique and need to treat yourself with respect. Continue to work on yourself and grow. Learn from your mistakes and continually get better.

One time I started a new job, and during the orientation, my boss went around the room and everyone was to introduce themselves and tell something interesting about themselves and share a favorite hobby. As they started sharing, I was not listening to my new coworkers talk about themselves. I was trying to think of something to talk about. I did not know what I liked to do. I knew I liked reading to my son. Playing with my son. Making food for my son. But myself? I had no clue. I was embarrassed to speak and so full of it when I did share. I faked a bunch of hobbies when I spoke to fit in. In reality, gosh, I was going through the motions, doing what I had to do to stay afloat and finding joy and laughter when it came. I had completely lost myself.

This is not good, and I will tell you how I learned the hard way. I do love being a mommy. It is by far my favorite part of my life. But I regret not working on and caring for myself like I cared for my son. If I did, I would have been a better mom because I would have been a happier person.

Know yourself and find yourself. Your babies will grow up. They will get all cool and stuff and want to hang out with their friends more than their mom. Then what? If we are not strong in who we are as an individual, we become lost. This happened to me. I didn't know who I was anymore without small kids that needed my presence twenty-four seven. So, as they grew more and more independent, I felt like I was nobody. My whole identity was them. I went through a severe depression in which I slept too much, I ate too much, and I drank too much.

One of my former students, Amanda, has two kids and is going to college pursuing her nursing degree. I am so proud of her and love the woman she has grown to become. Every week or two, she gets dressed up and goes out with friends. She is put down a lot by her family for doing this. They call her a bad mom and tell her she needs to be home with her kids every night.

People in my life did the same thing. If I was not home with my kids every single night, I was being a selfish person and a terrible mother. I couldn't even enjoy myself when I tried to have a life because I was filled with so much guilt and shame. I regret it.

I disagree with Amanda's family. I think her dedicating one night a week to enjoy herself makes her a good mom. She is confident in herself and is her own person with a life that she enjoys. When she is with her kids, she is happy and confident and enjoys them more because she is solid in who she is as a person.

Have you heard of married couples that have weekly date nights without their kids? It's pretty common. Are they terrible people for doing this? Society says it is okay for them to do it, to take time for themselves, and that it is healthy. Yet when a single mother enjoys a night to herself, she is considered selfish or neglectful of her children. I call bullshit. You don't have to lock yourself in your room and lose yourself because you are a mom. Take care of you, because YOU are important, too!

Chapter 11
CONSEQUENCES

OKAY, THIS IS A SHORT CHAPTER, BUT IMPORTANT enough to have its own section. A sentence I hear a lot from teen moms is, "Well, this is my consequence, so…" I used to say it, too. As an adult and a mom and a teacher, I will tell you that I throw up a little in my mouth every time I hear it.

Let me explain. Yes, you had unprotected sex, and yes, becoming pregnant is the consequence of your action. So, technically, your baby is your consequence. Okay, so let's get a little technical here. In my studies on applied behavior analysis, I learned all about behavior and functions of behavior as well as consequences. The consequences are good or bad, and they come as a result of everything we do. Literally, every action we take has a consequence, or a result.

This morning I got in my car, and the gas light came on. The consequence of me not filling my tank yesterday was that I would have to do it this morning and may be late for work and had to hurry. So, I stopped for gas, and the consequence of that was I got to work a few minutes late, but I got there, and now I am working. While I was at the gas station, I purchased a Diet Pepsi and a red chili burrito along with a lottery ticket. The ticket was not a winner, and the consequence was that I had five fewer dollars in my wallet and trash to throw away. It was way too early for a fried burrito, and the consequence was that my stomach hurt at work.

So, you see, every action we take, good and bad, has a consequence. These consequences help shape our behavior by motivating us to do or not do certain things. But we don't stop and bring up every good and bad consequence we face on a daily basis in our conversations. That would make you the weirdo in the room. The word consequence has a negative connotation, meaning it sounds yucky.

Think about it. How would you feel if you heard your mother explaining to everyone that your presence on this Earth was her consequence every day? Every time you bring up the fact that you made a bad choice, and your child is your consequence, you affect their self-esteem because you associate them with negative. So, unless you talk about every consequence you face on a daily basis, bringing up your child as a consequence is not necessary. If you wouldn't tell me you had a bite of ice cream at a birthday party, and as a lactose-intolerant person, the milk made you poop your pants, you don't have to tell me that you had sex and had a baby as a consequence. It is not necessary.

Conclusion

OUR LIVES ARE CHANGING FAST, AND IT CAN BE overwhelming to think about everything ahead of us. I want you to first and foremost know that you are not alone. As teen moms, we feel alone a lot. We are misunderstood and put down. It seems impossible. But there are millions of teen moms around the world and tons of them are successful and happy and have created wonderful lives for themselves and their child.

I want you to know that you can make it, too. When times get hard, I hope you pick up this book and find inspiration to continue on your path, push through the hard times, and to not give up or quit working diligently on yourself and your successful future. Take care of yourself first and treat yourself with love and respect and set boundaries that ensure the people in your life treat you with the same respect. When you take good care of yourself, you will be stronger and more patient and a better mother for your little one. You will also be stronger when those tough moments come, and when hateful people make the journey even harder.

Remember that co-parenting is hard for everyone. We broke up with our exes for a reason and probably harbor some resentment towards them. When your child is the focus of your attention and not the past and present disagreements, you will begin to somehow get along because you have a common goal: the love and wellbeing of your child.

Savor the joy of being a mother and the laughter and chaos that come with it. Enjoy the little moments and take time to make memories and cherish your little one and be thankful for the blessing they are in your life. I wish you the best of luck on your journey. I have been there, so I mean it when I say that it can be hard, but it is worth it to do it right. Us teen moms share so many of the same struggles. So from one teen mom to another: you got this!

PART II

Teen Parent Stories

THESE ARE TRUE STORIES OF REAL-LIFE TEEN moms at various stages of their journey. As you read, ask yourself if you want your story to be like the one you are reading. If so, what steps are you going to take? If not, what choices will you make that will make your story different? Listen to the advice given by these teen moms.

We have been there. We are telling you our stories because we have been there. We want you to be successful and want you to avoid making the same mistakes we made. We believe in you. The names have been changed for anonymity, and writing styles differ according to who is writing their story.

Chastity was one of my closest friends in high school. We had a lot of fun doing rebellious things together. She found out she was pregnant during our junior year of high school, just a few months before I got the news that would change my own life forever. I was one of the first people she confided in when she found out. She told me she had made up her mind and was going to have an abortion, that she was calling to make the appointment in the morning. She did not want to be a mom, did not want to raise a baby, and did not want any part of it at all.

At the time, I was completely against it and asked her to give me a week to talk with her about it, and at the end of the week, I would respect her decision and back off. I was on a mission to change her mind, and she respected my wishes as her friend.

When the week was over, she decided to go ahead and have the child. Her family was so very excited. They threw her a baby shower, and her mother was thrilled she was going to have her first grandchild. She had an abundance of support. Her parents were educated and had money and were there for her throughout the pregnancy. It was their first grandchild, so they were there for every part of her pregnancy journey.

Chastity was indifferent about being pregnant and seemed as though she was not really concerned with what was happening in her life. She continued to party while pregnant and after the baby was born. She never stopped doing things that we were doing before she found out that she was going to be a mom. She continued afterward. She would go to parties and take her baby and leave her child with whoever happened to be at the party and willing to take him. She started using drugs and seemed to spiral out of control. Her parents always had her baby, and she was out doing what she wanted.

We had a lot of super sketchy friends in high school. One night she was out with some of these friends, and someone shot a gun at some people they did not like in a nearby car. Eventually, Chastity was arrested and charged with attempted murder, even though she did not pull the trigger. She was there, and she was very much guilty. She was sentenced and went away to prison. Her son was placed with his father and was not living the best life. His father was shortly afterward deported out of the country for illegal activities, and as a result, the child went to live with his grandparents.

After his deportation, his father was diagnosed with AIDS and died soon afterwards. I have not heard anything about him since. Chastity was in prison for years, and her son was being raised by her parents. Life went on.

I have spoken to her son many times, and he says that his grandmother is his mom. He wants nothing to do with his biological mother. He says she is disgusting and an embarrassment. He has grown to be an amazing young man who joined the military and is happy with his own family now. He will not speak to his biological mother, and she has been released from prison with no family to return to.

Last time I saw Chastity, she was high on methamphetamine and did not mention any of her children. She had five since she was released from prison and got married. She still uses drugs and seems to have the same mentality she had the day she found out she was going to be a mom.

Growing up was rough. My dad was always in and out of prison. My mom went to college and became a pharmacy tech, and we were all really proud of her. She got a job, but soon fell into an opioid addiction. My dad got out of prison at this time when she became addicted. He was addicted to meth really bad.

One day we were at our condo in Visalia and my mom and dad were arguing, and he beat her up. I ran downstairs to try and help my mom and he beat me up, too. He went to jail for it and while he was in jail, my mom got fired for stealing the medication from the pharmacy she worked at, and we had to move back in with my grandma. She continued to take the medication, however, and it got really bad. We would find her passed out in the front yard and we would have to call an ambulance so that they could pump her stomach. She overdosed multiple times. My mom got her own apartment and started doing meth and heroine. I remember she had so much traffic in and out of the house all of the time. She would never care where I was or what I was doing.

When I was in seventh grade, I basically lived with a friend and her grandma because I liked it there, and my mom never cared where I was. She would only call every couple of weeks to ask me for favors. When I did go home, she would have so many druggies in and out of the house and would fight me. This was my life in seventh and eighth grade.

In eighth grade, I would also stay with another friend whose mom would take good care of me like I was her own daughter. When I would go home, my mom would get physical with me. We never had food because she would sell her food stamps for meth. My siblings and I would cry and tell her that we were hungry, and she would yell at us and tell us to make signs and go stand on the corner, holding them if we were really hungry and wanted food.

Then my dad got out of prison, and he changed his life around. He got clean, and I wanted to go live with him and get out of the environment I was in at my mom's. My mom was angry. She wanted my dad to take her back, and he would not, and she would keep us away from him and not allow us to see him. She would threaten us if she thought we were going to see him or talk to him.

One time I visited him, and she got mad and sent me to my room, telling me that I was now her prisoner and could never leave the room. I had to ask permission to go to the restroom and to even to sleep. After a couple of days of this, I ran away. I just wanted to live with my dad, but she had so much hate towards him because he left her. I lasted a couple weeks until the police found me and took me back to my mom. She would follow me around the house because she thought I was going to do it again. We started fighting, and my grandma's Pitbull went to attack her for hitting me, and she grabbed me and pushed me in front of the dog to protect herself. When the police got called, again, CPS got involved. They took us away from my mom.

We were in foster care until they gave my siblings back to my mom but let me go with my dad. My dad continued to fight for custody of my siblings and eventually got some. My mom only had supervised visitation at this point. During one of the visitations with my mom, my little brother was given a bottle with meth in it and drank it. My mom was sentenced to six years for this, and I have not spoken to her since.

I met my kids' dad through some mutual friends and would see him around all the time. We eventually started talking and from then on, we were together. I planned to have my first baby. I felt like a baby was what I was missing in life. I wanted her to fill the piece of my heart that was missing. I was so happy when I found out about her. When I told my family, they all told me I needed to go have an abortion. Every time I was around them, they would constantly bring up that this is what I needed to do.

One of the hardest parts of being a teen mom was that people were so mean and judgmental to me, even my own family. The best part was that I knew I always had someone to love and who would love me back the same. I had a forever best friend. I don't have any regrets because I feel that my struggles made me strong.

I would tell other teen moms to never give up. Even when you feel alone or when you are going through a lot, always remember that your baby is watching you, so you can't give up. Things will get better.

My life right now is a beautiful struggle. I am in college and have my own apartment with my kids. I have two more years before I am finished. I know I will finish and set a great example for my kids.

When I was three, my dad left my mom and me. We lived alone for about a year until she met my stepdad. He was cool but he had a bad drug problem and really bad anger issues. He couldn't really hold down a job, and a couple times we had to live out of his truck when we became homeless. When he was on drugs, he was okay, but it was when he was coming down or didn't have any drugs that he was terrible. I would refuse to leave the house because I felt like I needed to be with my mom and defend her.

My step-grandfather was molesting me. My dad got sober, and I told them what was happening to me. My grandparents were paying for us to live in a motel since my dad got clean, so when my parents discussed it, they decided they needed the help they were getting from him, and that I must be lying. My stepdad would call me a liar and tell everyone that I was a liar and would be until the day I died so not to listen to me talk. We continued to go to my grandparents like nothing had happened, and the family decided I was lying.

My dad was bad on drugs and abusive in the beginning, but my mom put up with it until he got clean. Eventually, when he got sober, my home life got much better. I, however, became much worse.

I started going out, hanging out with the wrong crowd, and partying a lot. I found out I was pregnant when I was fifteen years old. I was scared, so I went and had an abortion.

I thought about it all the time. I got pregnant again on purpose because I felt bad about the abortion and thought maybe my child had a second chance to be born again if I just got pregnant again. At that age, I thought it was the same kid, and I was making up for it. I later had another abortion and then had my son for the same reason.

When I had my daughter, it was the happiest day of my life. Her dad was under house arrest and stayed home while I went to the hospital and had her alone. I moved in with her dad, and it was bad. We would fight and he would beat me up all the time. When I came home from the hospital it got better for a few weeks, and then got bad again. He started going out all the time and would get violent with me. His mom came home a couple times while he was doing this and I was so relieved, thinking she would make him stop, but she would not get involved and minded her own business.

After three months, I decided to leave. I took my daughter and moved back in with my mom. It was wintertime, and there was no electricity or gas at her house, so it was really hard again. I am so glad she was just a baby and could not remember everything.

When my daughter was two, I met my son's dad. We went on our first date to the beach. I had always drank and took pills, but this was the first time I tried meth. I loved it. I kept doing it for a while and then quickly moved to heroine. I had gone to rehab and tried to get clean and was on methadone for the heroine withdrawals.

When I had my second child, his dad was in jail, so I did it alone again. My son was born with methadone in his system and was considered a drug exposed infant. Child Protective Services wanted to take the baby, but I begged for my son and after they spoke to my drug counselor at the methadone clinic, they agreed to let me take him home and try. I started working with CPS and taking classes and drug testing for them regularly.

I was about four months away from getting my son back, and I relapsed hard. I started slamming heroine and meth and quit going to my appointments. I got really bad really fast. About two months away from getting him back, I went to test, and it was dirty. I don't know how they knew that my daughter was at my mom's, but I got a call from her. She was crying and cussing and telling me they took my daughter from her. I still had my son, so I hid him in my garage. His grandmother came and got him from me and turned him over. She told me that I needed to get my shit together and this did not have to be forever, but it had to happen right now. I was so addicted. Without drugs I could not even get up to use the bathroom. I never got my kids back. I never quit doing drugs.

Years later I am still addicted. I have switched to fentanyl and have to smoke it at least three to four times a day. I wish so much that I could go back and change that day I went to the beach and tried meth for the first time.

I was at the park one time with a friend, and my daughter walked up to the playground with her grandma. I am not allowed to be around my kids. I did not know what to do so I hid under the table. That is the worst feeling you can have as a mother. I couldn't hug her. I couldn't say hi or even that I am sorry. It killed me. I tried going to rehab a couple times, but when I came out, I was homeless and frustrated and turned back to drugs every time.

Now, I live with my boyfriend. We are homeless and go from house to house when we can. He had his leg amputated from drug use, and we sit out at gas stations and panhandle for money to buy more drugs. We fight a lot. We fight over who gets the biggest half of the drugs we split. When we try and get sober, we fight more.

I am not happy, and I regret my life. I wish I could go back; I would change it all, starting with that day at the beach. I can't see my kids, I can't call them on birthdays, and I can't even tell you how old they are. Talk about being a piece of shit.

Their dads were doing the same things I was, but they got to see the kids because of their family. My daughter's dad overdosed and died, but my son's dad sees him all the time. It is so lame to be addicted to drugs and be in the same spot you were in ten years ago. I wouldn't wish this on my worst enemy.

My advice to other teen moms is to finish school. You can't do shit without a high school diploma. You can go to college and get paid to go to school after you get it, so get it. Watch who you surround yourself with. The people around you make a big difference in the choices you make. Drugs seemed normal because everyone was doing them.

I hope you never know how I feel because you make better choices and get your kids in your life. There is no such thing as a functional addict, and there is no trying drugs when you want to try them. They take over. Being a teen mom is hard, but trying to numb the pain hurts more in the end. Don't give up, and work hard for your kids. They are all we have.

My childhood was okay. My parents both worked a lot, and I had everything I needed financially. I missed out emotionally, but I had a roof over my head and food to eat, so I couldn't complain. I was fifteen when I found out I was pregnant. I was very small, about a hundred pounds. I didn't show, so I hid the pregnancy until I was about five and a half months. I told my baby's dad, and he left. He had two other girls pregnant at the same time I did not know about. I had to get a paternity test to prove to him it was his child. He didn't have anything to do with my son, though. He never knew my son or tried to know him.

I was daddy's girl. I loved my dad. Our relationship fell apart for years after I told my dad. My mom and I became estranged as well. She was mean and put me through a lot. She wanted me to have an abortion and told me over and over again that I ruined my life and would never amount to anything. She said my dad would never look at me the same, and that hurt me because I loved my dad so much.

I started working as soon as I found out I was pregnant because I was positive my parents would kick me out. They wouldn't really speak to me, so I spent a lot of time at one of my friend's houses.

I had my son, and everything changed. I was motivated. I was strong. I became a CNA by the time I was a junior and was taking college classes in my senior year of high school.

My friends and I were all headed in the wrong direction, and I never felt like I had a purpose. Until my son.

The hardest part of being a teen mom was realizing I was no longer a kid, and it was time to grow up. I lost a lot of friends and was alone all the time. But the best parts were way better than the hard parts. I wanted to be a good mom, and I loved my son so much that I took my life in a different direction.

Now I have four kids, two businesses, and took in a foster child to help out and give back. I'm happy. My son is going to college to become the first doctor in our family, and it makes me so proud when I think about him and that I must have done something right.

The advice I would give other teen mommies would be to know that you will lose friends. You will feel sad and alone at times, but it will be okay. Surround yourself with people who are motivated and with other mommies who are working hard for their families, too. When you get looked down on and feel judged, try and keep your head up and keep going. Work hard, love your baby, and be a good mom and you will make it and be okay.

Christy stated to me that she is willing to share her story with other teen moms and wants to help them but that she still could not discuss all that she has gone through out of respect for her own children and fear of starting drama in her family. Partly because they don't know everything and partly because they would not be comfortable with her sharing or making them look bad.

She met her child's father when she was only fourteen years old. He was eighteen. Growing up, she was continuously sexually abused as a child, and she so desperately wanted to take control of her life. So, she thought that being an adult was a way to take control, and she could start being an adult by being in an adult relationship. So that is what she did. She was seventeen when she found out that she was going to be a mom. She missed her period and felt that she was pregnant. She was right. She was on birth control at the time, so she was confused. She was also taking medication for other health problems, however, and this made her birth control less effective, and she did not know.

She was terrified to tell her mother. She didn't know how her mother would respond. She waited until her mother was in a great mood. Her mother was decorating the house and cleaning and seemed happy. It seemed like the right time, so she told her. When she told her mother, her mom immediately turned bright red and was furious. Christy was terrified. The first words that came out of her mom's mouth were that she was so disappointed in her daughter. Her mother was very concerned with appearances and immediately worried about what others would think of the family now. She was unhappy about the damage that would be done to the family's reputation moving forward. She decided that Christy was to get married immediately to help and make them not look bad. At seventeen, Christy did not want to get married yet. She was only seventeen, and it scared her. At that age, she did not know how to voice her concerns or say no. So, she said okay to please her mother.

Before the wedding, her father took her to his friend who was a judge. The judge asked her if she was sure she wanted to be married. She looked at her father and said yes when he nodded yes to her. She was afraid to say no. Her mother took her to the priest of her church, whom she was required to talk to before the wedding. She was told that in order to be a Catholic of good standing, she was to marry this man. If she did not, it was not okay with her religion. Again, she was terrified.

Christy was miserable and lost. She was before she became pregnant, but it just seemed to get worse during her pregnancy and when her child was born. She decided to take her child to a daycare and stay in a traditional high school, finish school, and earn her diploma. She said that she returned to find that things were very different at school and that very few people were nice to her now. She had a lot of friends before, but now felt really alone. She had a lot of good friends she was excited to return to and see and tell them about her baby. She was surprised when many of them told that they were no longer able to speak to her or be friends with her. Either their parents would not allow it, or they did not want to be associated with her kind of girl.

Soon after she started school, she started having some health problems from having the baby and switched to homeschooling. She was telling her mom and other adults in her life that she was in a lot of pain, and was told things like, "What did you expect? You had a baby." She was told that she should have thought about that before she decided to have a baby and to just deal with it.

One day, Christy started eating a grilled cheese sandwich and choked. When she choked, she coughed, and blood began pouring down her legs. She was scared and ran to her mother. Her mother said she would not take her to a doctor, she did not feel it was necessary. Instead, she would call her friend, who was a nurse, and have her stop by the house to check her out. The nurse told her mom that Christy needed to get to the hospital immediately. She had serious complications and needed professional care for her episiotomy immediately. There was no other choice, and there was no keeping this a secret.

Christy's husband began using drugs regularly and was not very helpful to her at all. She felt alone. Even worse than before, and he was getting more and more addicted. Her life was getting worse and more out of control. She stated that looking back, she did not think that he was a terrible person but that he, too, felt pressured to get married too young. He was not happy either and was also struggling just to get by. She described her marriage and her life at that time as horrible. She eventually divorced her child's dad when her child was two. She felt completely alone from the ages of fourteen to twenty-one.

When she got a divorce, she moved in with her mother and went to cosmetology school. She learned how to do hair and nails and had a blast. It was the first time she had to commit to leaving her child at a daycare center, and this was really hard for her. She worked days and went to beauty school at night, so she missed her child all the time. She met her second husband and decided she wanted to be home with her child, so she started her own daycare and worked at home.

Christy divorced again and decided to start over and start college. At this time, she was a single mother of three children, and it was hard. She still was not happy, but she still was not going to quit or give up.

She is glad that she stayed in college and worked toward her teaching credentials and her new career. Her kids are now all grown now, and there is a lot of love between them all. Her children respected her because they saw her struggle and knew how hard she was working to provide for them.

The hardest part of being a mom for Christy was that people were so mean and judgmental to her. She felt alone and felt like the places you were supposed to go for support and love she had instead received judgment and shame. She did not even realize that so much of this was happening until she was older and looked back at her life.

The best part of being a young mom was that she had so much energy. She frequently took her kids on bike rides, and they did a lot of fun things together, which strengthened their relationship.

Her advice to all the young moms out there is to keep moving forward. Ignore the negative. Even when it is hard. Understand that people don't understand us and will react certain ways to us, but we must make a conscious effort to ignore the negativity, or it will eat you up and ruin your life. Don't stop moving forward or trying to figure things out about your own life and past.

MARIA, AGE 22

I grew up poor and in poverty. When I was little, my mom moved to Washington and took my three older siblings with her but left me with my grandma and grandpa. They were forced to raise me. My grandpa was deaf, so I couldn't interact or communicate with him and was raised by my grandma. In school, I was a good student. I never got in trouble at school, and I tried really hard, and I was really smart.

When I was in middle school, my mom came back, so I went to live with her. She did a lot of drugs, and she didn't really care about how I did in school, so I quit caring, too. I changed a lot when I went back to live with her. I was so scared when I found out I was pregnant and didn't tell anyone but my older sister. One day, my sister got into an argument with our mom and yelled, "Well, Maria is pregnant!" My mom got so mad and told me I was going to have an abortion. I didn't want to and said no. I had to move in with my sister because if I lived with my mom, I would have had to have an abortion, and I didn't want to. I wanted my baby.

The hardest part of being a teen mom for me was that I did not have any idea how to take care of a baby. I hate learning by making mistakes, and I do that a lot as a mom. The best part is that I have little human beings I love so much and who love me so much.

My advice to other teen moms would be that everything will come in time, and that it is okay to make mistakes as long as you learn from them. You can be a good mom if you want to and try to be.

PASSION, AGE 34 AND TRISH, AGE 47

I met Passion at a homeless encampment in a town I used to live in. I knew of the encampment because my son and I had taken food out there a couple of different times on the way home from holiday dinners. I drove by and she was sitting on a couch in the middle of a dirt field. I slowed down and asked if she minded if I came and talked to her for a minute to write down her story to share with other teen moms.

You see, Passion was a teen mom. She was living in a homeless camp with her mom, who was also a teen mom. It was hot, and she was sitting on a couch with a makeshift umbrella. Passion was so welcoming and loving from the day I met her. She let me sit and visit and ask her questions about her life. I often visit her and check on her.

She has a hard life. I have tried to offer her money, but she refuses every single time. She said at that time they needed my prayers and did want my money. They both shared their life stories, and I was amazed at how much they had been through and that they still had smiles on their faces and love in their hearts to share all they had to give, their life stories, with other teen moms.

Trisha did not know she was pregnant with Passion until she went into labor. She had been using drugs and drinking heavily and did not realize she was with child. Passion was two pounds when she was born and was taken from her mom when she tested positive for substances.

Trisha said that for the first time in her life, when she saw her daughter, she felt what true love felt like. All she wanted was her baby. She did everything that she was to do and got her child back. She still struggled, but with her daughter by her side.

Passion grew up with her mom, who struggled with drug addiction and severe mental health issues, and Passion says that her mother has chased men and drugs the majority of her life. She always worked and always provided what she could, but Passion said that she very much raised herself. She said she was also raised by the streets. She partied and gangbanged and ran away frequently. She would hear from the streets that her mom was going through things and would go home to help her. When her mom was settled, she would run away again.

She was a teen and was living in a homeless shelter with her mom when she found out she was pregnant. She was told to have an abortion but chose to keep her child. She had him and said that she, too, for the first time, felt the true love of being a mom. She was out partying and gang-banging and active in her street life. She had her son and continued that life as it was all she knew. She said she loved the streets, and it was all she needed. She eventually got sick and was diagnosed with a disease that would one day leave her in a wheelchair and then lead to her death. This scared her son's father, and he left the state and left her with her son.

She had been living in a small home with her son and her mom for nine years and was then given notice that the property was being sold and they would have to move. They couldn't find a home and moved to a homeless shelter. She had to send her son to live in a different state with his dad because she could no longer provide for him and would eventually die from her disease. She hated the shelter and moved to a tent on the side of the road, which is where I met her and her mom.

She cries when she talks about her son and how much she loves him. She wants him with her, but it is better for him to go with his dad. She lives in a tent with very few belongings, one of them a large picture of her son.

Passion's advice to other teen moms was to love your baby with all you have. Don't give them up or give up on them because others tell you that you should. It is hard. But it is the only true happiness that she has ever felt in her entire life. Her son is the only person on this Earth that has never let her down. She is selling drugs and saving her money and sending it to him as she can. He took his girlfriend to prom, and she was so proud that she was able to send the money to pay for their dinner. She is so proud that her son treats his girlfriend with respect and is not living her street life. Her main concern in life right now is what will happen to her son when she dies. She has nothing to leave him and worries that he will be okay.

In 2013, I was a fifteen-year-old freshman in high school. It was March, second semester, and the beginning of the end of the school year. Little did I know, it was also the beginning of the end of my "normal" teenage life.

I was in geography class and was falling asleep on my iPad. I didn't know what was going on with me. I was on a full night's sleep, and nothing had changed in my routine. I turned around to talk to my friend, who sat behind me and told her (jokingly) that I thought I was pregnant.

She laughed and said, "Why?"

I, still joking, said, "I am so sleepy and tired. Let's look up pregnancy symptoms!"

Using our school-provided iPads, we started to search Google for the earliest pregnancy symptoms. I knew that it was a possibility because I had been having unprotected sex with my boyfriend at the time, but I didn't think it could happen to me. Isn't that what we all think until it happens to us? Of course, at the top of the list was a missed period, sleepiness, and nausea. That's when I began to get scared, but I still didn't want to accept that this could be happening to me.

"Dude, you're so pregnant!" my friend whispered.

I laughed it off and said, "Well, I guess I'll take a pregnancy test and see what happens."

After school that day, I went to my boyfriend's house. To make things worse and make my anxiety skyrocket, we were on a "break." We had been for weeks, and now I was showing up at his door, saying, "*Hey, dude, I think I'm pregnant and you're the dad!*"

I was embarrassed about not only potentially being pregnant at fifteen but telling this boy who wasn't even my boyfriend anymore that I could be having his baby in a few months. What if he didn't believe me? What if he thought that I was sleeping around and was trying to pin this baby on him?

He answered the door, looked down at me, and smiled. "What's up?"

Not much, I'm just here to change—and possibly ruin—our lives.

"I think we need to go to the doctor."

He gave out the most nervous giggle, and without needing any explanation, he said, "Fuck… Okay, when do you want to go?"

I told him to meet up with me the next day after school, since it was an early-out day. I wanted to go straight to a doctor, because I knew it would be confidential and did not want to risk being seen by anyone purchasing a pregnancy test at the store. We were pretty well known in our small town, and word traveled fast—especially when it was about teen pregnancy. As if the situation couldn't get any worse, when we got to the clinic, I noticed that the nurse working at the front desk was none other than my mom's close friend! I didn't even know she worked there!

I walked up to the desk and asked to speak to her in private. She led me into a hallway behind the front desk and asked what was going on. I had to tell her the truth but asked that she not tell anyone, or I would get her fired for breaking "patient-doctor" confidentiality (whatever that meant in my fifteen-year-old mind). She agreed to give me a pregnancy test for free without even signing in, just to make sure that no one found out that I was there.

Looking back at it now, I see how far above and beyond she went to help me out. She could've potentially lost her job for me!

Anyway, she had me pee in a cup and wait in the restroom for her to come back with the results. About five minutes later, I heard her knock on the door, and I let her in. She looked at me with such an empty, shocked stare and said the words I was dreading to hear, "Miriam, you are pregnant."

I don't exactly remember what my reaction was to that statement. All I remember is walking back out of the restroom and into the lobby where my newly found baby daddy was waiting. Again, I didn't even have to say a word. He gave me the same nervous giggle and said, "You're fucking pregnant, aren't you?"

When I'm uncomfortable, all I can do is smile and giggle—but it doesn't necessarily mean I'm happy. During our entire walk back home, all I could do was giggle and cry a little inside. My entire life flashed before my eyes and all I could think was, *"Oh my god, I'm going to have a whole baby!"*

Not once did we consider *not* keeping the baby. After all, we knew that this was a possibility and that we needed to be held accountable for our actions.

FAST FORWARD TO NOVEMBER

As my due date, November 16th, got closer, the emotions ran higher, and the anxiety grew worse. After many months of crying and refusing to believe that this was my reality, and I was going to become a mom, I finally accepted it. I was excited. I was excited to know that I was going to have this little human in my life that would change my life forever and for the better. I spent countless hours on Amazon, looking for cute little outfits for my baby girl and hoping that one day, once I finished school and had a job, I would be able to afford them. I ended up getting home-schooled because I felt like an oddball in my classes, and as my belly grew, the desks just kept getting less and less pregnant-teen friendly.

I went into labor on November 18th, at around three in the morning and didn't tell a single soul, other than my boyfriend-slash-baby-daddy. I was in so much pain, but I didn't want to go to the hospital because I didn't want them to send me back home. If I was going to be in pain, I wanted to be in the comfort of my own room and in my own bathroom. I distinctly remember calling my seventh-grade teacher, Mrs. Jones, and telling her what I had been feeling and how bad the pain was. She helped me time my contractions over the phone and when she realized they were less than five minutes apart, she told me to get my butt to the hospital, or I was going to have that baby at home.

The hospital was thirty minutes away from where we lived, so the ride there was awful! I was so uncomfortable and in so much pain. By the time I got checked in and the nurses checked my cervix at around eight thirty P.M., I was already eight centimeters dilated. EIGHT FREAKING CENTIMETERS! The nurse asked if I wanted an epidural, and I said heck yes! I had been dealing with the pain for so long, I just wanted it to stop. Well, good thing she did give me the epidural. My baby's heartrate started to drop, and I wasn't able to push her out, so they rushed me into an emergency C-section. To sum it up, I dealt with the pain of labor for seventeen hours, only to be cut open anyway! Fun times!

I welcomed my baby girl, Aubree, at two thirty-three A.M. on November 19th. I finally felt purpose in life. I looked at her and all I could do was cry and apologize to her for ever feeling like I didn't want her. For even during darker days, hoping I would miscarry. For wishing I had never been pregnant in the first place and my life was still fun, free, and wild.

This was my true, first love. So deep, so unexplainable, and so incomparable to anything I had ever felt before. This love was unconditional. This was a mother's love for her child!

Every day, we were together. I hated having to leave her every week for just an hour to go turn in my homework at school. I vividly remember being at school and having to leave her at home with her daddy and hating it! I wanted to be there with her so badly for every second of her little life. She was my best friend, and to be quite honest, she was my everything.

When I first found out I was pregnant, I felt my world collapsing and I thought my life was over. Now, I had accepted that my life was just beginning alongside my little girl! All the pieces of my world were finally coming back together, and I was seeing my true purpose in life...

And then my world collapsed again. On March 10th, my sweetest Aubree passed away. There were no signs, there was no warning; she was just gone.

I had put my baby girl down for a nap. It was around noon, and I had some cleaning to do around our room. She was three months old and was outgrowing all her newborn clothes, so it was time to switch those out for three- to six-month clothes. By the time I was done putting all her newborn clothes in bags to get rid of, it was around two o'clock, and I noticed she was still sleeping, so I got in the shower. I got out of the shower, and her dad took a shower after me. We were planning to just hang out and watch TV until she woke up, then play with her.

At around four P.M. I sat on my side of the bed, which was about three feet from Aubree's crib. She was still asleep, and I found it odd because usually her naps were two to three hours long. I told her dad to get up and check on her, and in true teenage boy fashion, he gave me an attitude and said, "Why don't you get up? You're closer to the crib."

"Please, just get up and check on the baby," I said. I don't know what it was. It was like I wanted to check on her, but my body just would not react.

He got up and walked across the room. He stopped in front of her crib, picked her up, and yelled, "Miriam, the baby isn't waking up!"

I started freaking out and yelling at him to wake her up, and she just wouldn't. He lay her on our bed, and I saw her little blue body; it almost looked bruised. My heart knew she was gone, but my mind didn't want to believe it. I held her, and she was stiff and cold. My baby girl was gone. My first, true, unconditional, endless little love was gone. We called 911, and they took her to the hospital to hook her up to a bunch of machines and wires that I knew nothing about. There were so many doctors and nurses in that room, asking me so many questions that I cannot remember.

One nurse in particular that I do remember, however, came up to me and asked, "What's her name?"

"Aubree Zandalee," I said while trying to look past her and over her shoulder to see what they were doing to my baby girl.

"Aubree Zandalee," she repeated. "That's beautiful."

Still looking over her shoulder, I noticed wires were coming off her and machines were being unplugged.

"I'm so sorry, sweetie. Aubree has passed away. We couldn't bring her back."

I don't remember anything else after that. I remember so many people talking to me and asking me questions, but I don't know what their questions, or my answers, were. I remember sitting in a chair beside her hospital bed and asking to hold her. I don't know how long I held her for, but I remember looking at her and she just looked like she was asleep. She looked like her but didn't feel like her. She was cold and stiff—gone. My life flashed before my eyes, just like it did the day I found out I was pregnant. My world crashed again. My life was purposeless again.

The days leading up to her funeral were the most confusing to me. Just a week prior, I had a happy, healthy baby girl, and now, not only did I not have her, but I was planning her burial. I couldn't understand how this could be the outcome of my life. I thought about the other girl in my grade who had been pregnant around the same time as me. She lived in a trap house with her drug-dealing mom, she was a massive pothead before, and maybe even after, her pregnancy, and her baby was fine. Meanwhile, I was dealing with losing my baby girl, even when I had a stable, happy home for her. Why did she deserve her baby more than I deserved mine? What did my baby ever do to deserve death? She was an angel!

After her burial, I was in a depressive state. The thing about depression is that you never know what you're going to get. Some people cry all day and every day, some people eat their emotions away and pretend to be happy, and some even become suicidal. For me, depression was quiet. I was locked in a room, in bed, without talking to anyone. Occasionally, I would cry in the shower before bed and then start the next day the same way. I didn't leave the room unless there was no one in the house, and if I heard anyone pull up to the driveway, I would run to the room like a rat in the middle of the night. I didn't want anyone feeling bad for me, and I definitely didn't want anyone asking me questions and opening the door for conversation and tears.

I knew that I wasn't the only one hurting. My mom was hurting for me and for the loss of her first and only granddaughter. My grandparents were hurting for my mom's loss, their own loss, and mine. The pain they must've felt still tears in my heart. I was at a point where I could either work on healing myself and, as a result, help ease some of my family's pain, or I could stay in this depression and keep going in a downward spiral.

I chose healing. I chose to accept the loss that I was forced to deal with and to start praying. I went to my daughter's gravesite, and I cried for hours. I told her how much I loved her, how much she meant to me, and how much I wished she was still with me. I asked her for forgiveness if I ever did something wrong. I told her that she was such a good baby, that God deserved to have her closer to him. Her purpose on Earth was fulfilled with me, and now it was time for her to fulfill her purpose in Heaven. She is now my guardian angel.

Seven years later, here I am, in one of the best mindsets I have had in a long time, working at a job that I actually enjoy, married to my first and only baby daddy, and with a two-year-old baby girl named Mercie Annalee. I refuse to become a "product of my environment," as the people in the valley like to call it. I took all my unfortunate circumstances and put them in God's hands and manifested the life I would've wanted to provide for my sweet Aubree. I am nowhere near where I want to be, but I'm one step closer. Once you've hit rock bottom, there is only one way out, and that is upwards.

It is insane to think about how much of an impact my angel girl made on my life and my heart. Every time I am stressed out with this wild toddler of mine, I can almost feel Aubree talking to me and telling me to be patient, to enjoy all the little moments, just like I did with her. I think that what really got me through those difficult times was knowing that I spent every hour of my baby girl's life beside her. I enjoyed all the little moments and never complained about it. Yes, I cried with her a couple of times because I didn't know what I was doing, but I embraced it, and I kept trying. She made me a better mother for her baby sister, and I will make sure that Mercie knows that. I will make sure she loves her sister just as much as her sister loves her.

GABRIELLA, AGE 19

My name is Gabriella and I'm seventeen years old. Life for me growing up wasn't the best. I went through a lot at a young age. My mom brought me and my siblings to America because she wanted us to have a better life. My dad stayed in Mexico, and we moved to Avenal, California, when I was four in 2008. My dad ended up passing away in Mexico in 2015. From there I felt that I changed a lot, because I was always daddy's girl. I wouldn't get off the couch for days and started slacking in school.

When I was thirteen years old, my siblings and I were taken into foster care due to my mom going to prison for three and a half years and then jail for about eight months. When I got into foster care, I ran away and was on the run for about a year. I used to gangbang and fight a lot. I ended up getting a boyfriend, and I moved in with him while I was on the run. He was one of my homies and we ended up dating. Four months into the relationship, I found out I was pregnant at fourteen. I felt that it was for the better because I always told myself that if I get pregnant, I'm turning myself in.

Before I got pregnant, I had gotten locked up with four charges. When I found out I was pregnant, I turned myself in and changed my whole life around. I don't really have a family besides my aunt and uncle. They supported me. My mom was deported, so I had to let her know through text. She supported me. The hardest part about being a teen mom was being judged and not doing whatever I wanted to do because, obviously, I was a teen and wanted to do teen things. But I thank God for giving me a baby because I was doing badly in life, and when I found out I was pregnant, everything changed.

I wanted nothing but the best for my baby because I didn't have the best. I knew my son was going to have it all. Whether I was a teen mom or not. The best part about being a mom is you can't get bored when you have a little buddy to do everything with. I don't have any regrets. Things happen for a reason.

My advice to other teen moms is don't focus on the bad stuff, focus on the good stuff. Give your kid a better life than you had and don't give up on your little one. Me and my son are eighteen and three now, living our best life. My baby's dad and I are still together after three years. His family is really involved and helps us a lot. I am really thankful for them.

My mom was living in Mexicali, and she was a maid and got pregnant with my brother. The guy and his family were horrible to her because they had money, and she was just a maid, so she took my brother and moved. She came to the United States and started a new life where she met my dad and had my siblings and me. My dad had money, but he was extremely abusive to my mom and to us. He would travel to Mexico often because he had land and business there.

One time, he went to Mexico, and his brother was getting beat up by people in the drug business. My dad defended his brother and was shot and killed. My mom was single again, and she met my sister's dad and started a relationship with him. My life got worse when she met him. My entire family was sexually abused by him as well as by the other men in his family. It was ongoing and horrible and happening to all of us, the girls and the boys, in our house.

I remember at DARE (Drugs and Alcohol Resistance Education) we learned about sexual abuse. I came home and told my mom what was happening to us, and I got in trouble from my mom. They continued for years.

One night, he kidnapped a girl at a bar and raped her, so he went to prison. Once he was gone, I then told the school what was happening, and charges were pressed for that, too. My mom didn't leave him. She would take all of us to visit him in prison and we had to spend time with him. When he got sentenced for the abuse with us, she was angry with me.

She wanted to give me away so that she could live with him when he got out. I heard her talking with his mom one day. They were planning on leaving me with a family member in another town because I had told the school about the sexual abuse. We were never protected as kids. She ended up getting pregnant by someone else, so he dumped her from prison. He contacted HIV and died in prison.

Our life moved on. Eventually, through a mutual friend, I met my son's dad. He was cute and funny, and we started dating. I was hanging out with my friend at her house, and we had pregnancy tests, so I took one just for fun. The test said I was pregnant, so I was really confused. I was fifteen. Her mom was a social worker, so we took the test to her to ask what to do. Her mom took me to get medical care and helped me apply for insurance. I didn't tell my mom, but she figured it out. She slapped the shit out of me multiple times. She was not supportive; she would call me names and tell me all the time that I should not have opened my legs any chance she got. She never bought even one thing for my son. I had friends, and they helped me out, but nothing from my mom.

My son's dad started using drugs and meth and it got really bad. I was the only one working. I had my own apartment and car by the time I was eighteen years old. I would kick him out of the house sometimes and come home from work, and he would be hiding under my bed or in a closet. I still don't know how he got in. The neighbors would call the police all the time when he was yelling, but he came back, and I would eventually cave in and take him back. I really did love him, and he watched my son while I worked. One time I kicked him out and when I went to my car to go to work, he had written, "I love you, Tatiana, and if I can't have you, no one will! I promise!" on my car. I ignored all the red flags. It wasn't worse than my childhood, so it was still normal.

The final straw, though, was when I came home from work and decided I was done. I had done this before, so I probably wasn't sure at the time either. This time ended up being different. My best friend was with me. We had suspicions so we searched the entire house to see what he was up to. We found meth stashed in my son's toys, the attic, in and under the couches, and basically every place we looked. If it wasn't meth, it was the plastic that the meth was in when he had it. We looked everywhere. We even climbed and looked in the ceiling, and what we found was horrific. He had taken pictures of my little sister and cut them out and attached them to pornographic magazines. I was horrified and in shock and did not know what to do. My friend went to check the closet and when she did, there was no doorknob. She noticed something silver and pushed it. It was a knife. Someone was holding the door shut from in the closet with a knife.

My son's dad had been there the whole time and was watching us find out what he had been doing. We grabbed our kids and ran. The police couldn't find him when they came.

A couple days later my little brother was at my mom's, and my son's father fell through the roof of their house. He had been living in their attic since the incident at my house and had cut holes in all the rooms and was watching us. I put up with everything, but I could not let go of what he did to my sister's photos and finally left him for good. He got worse and eventually was put in jail for having sex with a twelve-year-old girl when he was like thirty. When he got out, he went on the run and was killed by police in a standoff in Texas.

I started going to church and working harder and working on myself. I quit putting out and stayed single for years while I focused on myself, my son, and my faith. I met my husband, and we got married and moved in together. I was so used to being independent and not having anyone to count on that I kept my apartment for months. I was scared to not have it. I would not give up my safety net.

We are still married now, and we have three kids together. My oldest son is now a father and works hard to care for his family now. I am happy and healthy and love my life. I cannot believe I ever was in a horrible relationship like my son's dad. My life is so different now. My husband took over his family business, and I work part time and teach dance classes at our local gym. I have a family now and I love it. The hardest part of being a teen mom was getting up, getting dressed, my son dressed, and dropping him off at the school daycare and going to school myself. I was always tired. I had bad grades and a hard time in school before my son. It was even harder after him, but I had to finish. The best part was he was so cute, and I loved him so much. Everyone I hung out with started doing drugs and crazy stuff, but I didn't because I had him. I was all he had and I would not do that to him.

I don't regret having him. What I do regret is that I deprived him of having a good dad by not waiting until I found the right person. My husband is such a good father, and he teaches my kids right and wrong. He is there, and he protects them like I never had growing up. My son didn't have that because I didn't choose a good dad for him.

My advice would be to stay single and to work on yourself. When you become strong and the woman you need to be, you will meet the right man who will treat you right. God will put him in your path when the time is right. Don't focus on what you don't have, focus on yourself and getting better in life and then you will have more.

NISREEN, AGE 17

My name is Nisreen and I have a two-year-old daughter. Growing up was fun for me. We would always be on the road with family to go visit family. We spent a lot of time together as a family. One day I was at the store and a boy who was really cute asked me for my Snapchat. I gave it to him and on February 1st he asked me out, and I said yes. I was dating him when I found out I was pregnant. I was using protection, but somehow, I still ended up getting pregnant. I felt happy when I found out I was going to have a baby. I always wanted one. I told my family right away when I found out. To tell them, I took them my ultrasound and told them I was pregnant. They were really mad at me at first, but eventually they got over it.

The best part of being a mom for me is watching my daughter grow and do new things. She is growing so fast. The only regret I have is meeting her father. We do not talk, and he is not a part of her life. The advice I would give other teen moms is that you can do it, and you will get through it even though it is hard.

My name is Areana V, and I am twenty-one years old. When I was growing up, I had a very hard time because I had a little brother who had cancer, so my mom was never there with us. She was always with him or taking care of him until he passed away.

I was fifteen years old when I got pregnant. I grew up knowing my child's father. We went to school together. I got pregnant because I never really used protection. I was scared to open up about it and ask for protection from anyone.

When I found out I was pregnant, my mom was with me. We had gone for a check-up and found out I was pregnant. I was really disappointed in myself because I was also very young. My mom was disappointed, but she was also my number one supporter through it all. The hardest part of being a teen mom was when I had to bring my son to school on the bus and had no help.

Even though I had a rough time, I do not regret my son. He is the best thing I have. Without him, I wouldn't be doing well at all. One piece of advice I would give teen moms is to talk to someone you trust so they can help with birth control or to have someone who supports you through it all and never give up. I graduated high school, and I am going to college, and I would not be here without my son.

I had a rough childhood. Growing up, we were poor, dysfunctional, and relocating often. I was raised by my maternal grandmother, lived with my dad and stepmom, and was sexually abused and treated differently than my other siblings. I was fourteen and living with my grandmother when I met my child's father. We lived in a large apartment complex downstairs, and a group of guys lived upstairs. They all knew my grandmother and would talk to her. One of them started talking to me and we started dating. He was much older.

On my fifteenth birthday we slept together and promised to be together forever. We got married two years later. I got pregnant at sixteen and had the baby a couple of months after my seventeenth birthday. I did not know I was pregnant until I went to the hospital in pain and was told that I was going to have a baby. I never found out like other moms. I passed the finding out, and I never knew until I went to the hospital for pain, and they checked me, and I was told that I was about to give birth. I was very scared and nervous. I was scared to tell my mom. My husband called and told my family while I was giving birth that I was pregnant and having a baby. Everyone was in shock, including myself. My mom was upset and wanted me to tie my tubes immediately.

The hardest part for me was that I was so worried if I was able to raise her and provide for her. After about a year and a half, her father and I broke up. I was worried that I could not do it alone, and when she got sick, I would worry that I would not have enough patience to handle caring for a sick child.

The best part of being a teen mom was the love I felt. I love her so much and I loved that after I gave birth, she belonged to me. I would dress her up in the cutest clothes, and I loved her so much. I have no regrets at all.

The advice I would give to other teen moms is to just do the best you can and be patient. It is a lot of work, especially when babies get sick or cry. You can definitely get overwhelmed at times. Ask family for help if you need it and remember that you can do it. I don't have a very exciting life now. I had five other kids, and one of them has special needs. I spend most of my time caring for him; it is much more difficult now that he is older. I also care for my grandkids. I love my baby I had as a teen and we have a great relationship now. She is married and has her own family now. Good luck on your journey of being a teen mom. You can do it!

Life growing up was good. My child's dad and I met when I was in school. I ended up getting pregnant by him when he came over to see me on my birthday. I felt scared and told him about it and we decided to keep on going with the pregnancy. It took me two months to tell my and his family until I ended up going to the hospital. My mom was disappointed but happy. His family was disappointed.

The best part of being a teen mom is having a little mini human that becomes a part of your life, and you don't have to be lonely anymore. I do not have any regrets. My life now is okay, but I get sad watching my little girl grow up. My daughter and I live with her dad, who is my boyfriend.

The advice that I would give another teen parent is to become strong for any challenges that are on the road for you, and never give up, even when you're tired of life. Just keep going, especially because of your child. They need you to be strong.

TINA, AGE 40

Growing up was chaotic. My parents divorced when I was eight and I lived with my mom in the low-income apartments in my town. My dad was not really available and did not work. I was not close with my mom's family, either. The only person I was close to was my grandma on my dad's side. She was like my mom. She did everything for me. She is still here with me to this day. My mom was always busy and never had money, so my grandma was the one who took me to practices, took pictures of me, and spent time with me.

I was sixteen and a half when I found out I was pregnant. My mom was in the hospital, and I took a test in the bathroom at the hospital. I was absolutely terrified. I did not have the best relationship with my parents, so I was scared to tell them. I was scared to tell my family, too. I knew they would be disappointed in me. I was a straight-A student and had perfect attendance and I didn't want to let them down.

My mom was mad and disappointed. She was a teen mom and I think, looking back, that she knew how I was going to struggle and did not want this life for me. The nurse at the high school helped me tell my grandma. She was the one I did not want to disappoint. My grandma cried and cried. That was very hard for me. I did not want to let her down. I told my dad about three months later. I can't remember his reaction, but we were not close, so I didn't really care.

I went on independent study for six weeks after I had the baby and immediately went back to school. I took my daughter to the adult school daycare because they had a program for teen moms. I graduated with my class and finished school. The hardest part of being a teen mom was losing all my friends. Nobody wanted to hang out with me and my baby, they had more fun things to do. I just felt out of place in high school after I had my daughter. My grandma helped me by watching my daughter at night so that I could work.

Within a year after my daughter was born, her father and I broke up. We were too young. He was involved with my daughter throughout her life, but I was not thrilled with the choices he made as her father. The positives of being a teen mom was that I was motivated like I had never been before.

I always knew that I wanted to go to college but being a single mom pushed me to actually do it even when it was hard. I met other young moms, and I am still friends with them. I feel like I broke generational trends in my family. I went to college. I am very close with my daughter, and she went to college and was not a teen mom. I had such a great experience with my nurse having my baby that I went to college and became a nurse. I really connect with teen moms, and I love it when young moms come in and I get to be a motivation to them like I had when I was in labor.

The advice I would give other teen moms would be to just never quit. It may take us a little longer to reach our goals because we have to work and care for a baby, but we can get there. I was a nurse for over ten years before I got my BA degree. It was a personal goal for me, so I went back and did it. So don't stop, and remember that it takes time. I would also say to remember that you will get your time. I remember feeling like I was missing out on everything because all I did was work and be a mom.

But now my kids are grown, and I get to go do all the things I felt like I was missing out on. I get to go to bars, and go dancing with my husband, we go on vacations, and I actually have money to do it now. It's hard but it's worth working hard for the life you want!

FATIMA, AGE 18

Growing up, my life was good. My parents were separated when I was sixteen and that was hard, but I got through it. I met my daughter's father when we went to preschool together. I moved away and came back during high school, and we met all over again. We dated, and I was not on birth control. We used the pull-out method, and we trusted it and thought we were fine. When I found out, I was so scared of what my mom would think, and I was so worried about my future. How was I going to raise a baby and finish school? My boyfriend and I told our families together, but I was too scared of my mom to tell her, so I told my little brother, knowing he would tell her.

They were not mad, just a little disappointed because, obviously, they wanted me to wait until I was older. The hardest part was learning how to have a lot of patience. The best part of this was having her in general. I love her so much and I love being able to love her. I do not have any regrets. The only thing would maybe be to finish high school first, because it was hard. The advice I would give other teen moms would be to be patient. Your child needs you the most. We are good and happy and healthy in life now. We are living in an apartment and saving money to buy a house in the next couple of years.

MELISSA, AGE 18

Dear teen mom,

I grew up in a household where we are very supportive toward each other, and where we can all express who we are without anyone saying anything. My mom always taught me to be respectful, kind, and caring. She is the best person and has taught me a lot growing up until now. I was always the little girl who wanted everything pretty she'd see, and sometimes we couldn't afford what I wanted, but somehow my mom made a way to get it for me. I have six siblings and I'm the middle child, so it's five girls and two boys in total.

My mom always made a way of getting all of us what we needed, as well as my dad. He would always work, so he missed out on our school events such as awards, concerts, teacher conferences, etc. He will always be the hardworking dad I know. My mom was always there for it all, even if it was going to the hospital at three A.M. I will always be grateful to God and that woman for giving me my life.

In elementary school, I was always the student who got good grades and was student of the month and student of the year. My three older sisters and I always got perfect attendance at school and left home with the trophy every year at the awards. Elementary was such an easy stage of my life compared to now. Except for how in sixth grade—I believe I was in—I fell into the hospital for almost a whole week, scared for my life and thinking I was going to be gone because they thought I had meningitis. I was in basketball and softball, which I enjoyed at the time.

I met one of my best friends in the apartments we used to live in, who unfortunately passed away due to cancer. She was the most beautiful and nicest person I've met, and we would always be together, my sister, her, and me. Her laughter was the most memorable thing about her. I would cherish every moment with her. That was when I experienced my first heartbreak. I got the news at school when my mom was dropping me and my three older sisters off, but we were in the school parking lot when I got told the sad news. I could barely walk up off my feet to enter school. I was crying the whole day. Oh, how I miss her. Then I got through elementary school as strong as I could, still remembering her.

Then came seventh grade, where I started to notice who true friends are and are not. I feel like the older you grow the more you realize and the more mature you become. Well, nothing much happened in middle school. I was in a group called "Stand for the Silent," where I got to customize the shirts we wore.

My sister got pregnant when I was in middle school and my parents and family were really supportive toward her. But my mom always taught us that we really need to know a man in order to have a baby by him, or at least wait until you're married.

Then came high school, that was when I really matured. I lost and gained friends. My education wasn't the best.

COVID hit and we went online, and I didn't do much homework. I got a job, which was my first actual job, at KFC. It really drained me from doing school and work at the same time. I lost a lot of weight. I got depressed. And it was just really hard for me to cope with everything. I started going out with friends a lot more and I started doing things I shouldn't have been doing. I was very much influenced by friends, but my mother taught me better. I just didn't listen.

I lost my grandpa, and it was very hard for me to cope through school. I heard about an independent study school through a friend I used to have. I got into the school, and it was the best thing for me. I'm so glad I went to that school. I met really amazing teachers, like Mrs. Hoskins and Ms. Shannel. I don't know where I would be right now without them as well. I will forever be grateful that I met them.

I met my daughter's dad and found out I was pregnant months after we started dating because I had already met him before. My pregnancy was the most difficult thing I had to experience in my lifetime. I do not wish it on my worst enemy. The first month I didn't even know I was pregnant, but I had that feeling like I was. I remember my mom had picked me up from work and I told her I was feeling all these symptoms, and she thought it was just because of my period, but I normally wouldn't get symptoms when I was about to start. So, she said just to take the thought off our heads of me being pregnant. She took me to the store, and we bought a pregnancy test, and that's when I found out I was pregnant.

I wasn't really shocked because I already had that feeling that I was. But my mom was super supportive and all she said was, "What are you going to tell your dad?" That was what had me nervous at the time.

My older siblings found out I was pregnant and were supportive as well. They got me my cravings or made them. My nieces and nephews and my little brother loved me even more and were always next to me. I finally told my dad I was pregnant about two to three months, and he was supportive as well. We sat down on the couch, and I did all the talking because my daughter's dad was too nervous and felt nauseous.

Seeing my baby in my belly for the first time was a feeling I will never forget, a feeling of happiness and excitement. My relationship was rocky. It had many ups and downs while being pregnant. So, it was super difficult for me. I was already going through so much and I just couldn't cope with being in a relationship that caused me stress as well. So, we decided on taking a break. And that was the most difficult thing ever for a pregnant woman. Thank God I had my family there with me through it all.

I fell into a hard depression. I wasn't gaining any weight; I was just losing it. I lost about twenty or more pounds during my pregnancy and didn't gain anything. I didn't have the energy to do anything. I was just so hurt.

Feeling my daughter kick or move inside me was just the best feeling ever as well. She was just my motivation to keep going. But, obviously, having pregnancy symptoms like throwing up and anxiety and just so much more, all got to me. Then we agreed on getting back together and for some time, we were on good terms. Then I had my gender reveal, and most of his family showed up, even uninvited people, which really made me upset because it had to be something small, not big, and they were people I didn't even know.

And then once again we took a break, I believe, days later after the gender reveal. And honestly, it broke me even more because I'd like to say all guys are the same and there are always going to be girls in the way. It is up to that person to take control of the situation of doing good or bad. But unfortunately for me, that wasn't the case. His family was the problem; they brought girls around him on purpose, and he made the decision to either talk to them or not. Rumors got to me and really drained me.

I didn't know what to do anymore. I was in and out of the hospital and just didn't want anything to do with him. I was so heartless and heartbroken, thinking, "What did I do wrong?" But I didn't do anything wrong. It was him. It got to the point where I wasn't myself anymore. I couldn't forgive him. I wasn't answering any of his calls or texts. He didn't deserve me. None of his family checked up on me while being pregnant. They never asked how I or the baby were.

I found out I was having a girl. I was so excited. Then it just sucks when you have people saying so much about you, and it being people you were once friends with or even your boyfriend's mom and family.

Church really helped me a lot. I'm so glad I went to church and just let God take control of my life.

Then, I remember my child's dad offered to take me to one of her appointments and I really didn't want him to, because the love and trust and just everything wasn't the same anymore. I was so hurt and broken at the time. After that, we started talking even more, and I still wasn't sure about him. I was that hurt, and every time I saw him, I saw everything he did. Social media really got us. The "following guys and girls," the requesting, and just everything. I wasn't in the right state of mind, and my mentality was just so messed up because of him and his family. It's always going to be hard to get through moments like that.

So, I spent a few months without any real contact with him whatsoever. It was truly hard for me because all I could think about was my daughter. I really didn't want my daughter to be without her dad, so I decided to reply to him. It took a lot of courage to do that. All that trust was gone, and that love was fading away. But I knew if we ever got back together, then I wasn't going to be the same person I was and I wasn't going to give him the same love as before because it was just taken advantage of. I really wanted to experience a happy pregnancy, but if I'm being honest, I really didn't. And I feel so bad because my daughter didn't deserve any of that, because she felt everything I did.

Honestly, neither of us deserved all that pain. I couldn't eat or sleep or even drink water, and nothing was our fault;

men have to be stupid. But I really did want her to know her dad, even though he didn't deserve it. I just couldn't have the heart to be like them.

Then I was eight months along, and I had her—my beautiful baby girl. It was like everything in life didn't even matter anymore once I saw my baby girl. I just knew I wanted what was best for her. I thank God; He knew how much I needed her because before she arrived. My water broke at my house, and my sister took me to the hospital. I was only six centimeters dilated, and my baby's heartrate was going down, so I had to get an emergency epidural and C-section. I was very scared for our lives. I was just praying and praying for me and my baby to get through it. And my sister was the one who went with me to get my C-section and they made her wait out for a little.

The last thing I remember was me asking where my sister was and trying to get up from the bed because of how scared I was to get a C-section. Then I opened my eyes, and my sister held my baby and showed her to me. That's when I realized that my happiness was my daughter. I thank God for her most every day now because she is and forever will be my happiness.

I tried being a family again and gave her dad another chance and he changed a lot from how he was before. But if we're being honest, I'm still not the same person. I just feel like everything I went through just destroyed me, but it made me stronger, and it made me guard and protect my love and peace so I won't have to give it away to someone again just so they can easily destroy it. I want to let go and let God control my life, and that is what I'm working on.

It's still hard trying to forget about the past when you see that person every day. I will know when to open up again to that same person. It's not easy and never will be but if you want to be a family and if you want your daughter to have both parents happily, then you have to make that effort to leave everything in the past. Yes, it's hard when you know the type of person they are and what they are capable of. Don't ever believe words but actions, because it's true when they say. Actions speak louder than words, and true colors are only seen when someone is mad, drunk, or sad. Even true colors are seen when you have a baby by that person. That says a lot about a person, and you will eventually see.

Right now, I'm still trying to cope with forgetting about the past, the lies, the "love" he supposedly has given me, his family, and just him in general. There will be plenty of arguing and assuming in a relationship, but that phase isn't forever. We decided to get rid of social media and that helped a lot as well. But I'm still learning how to be a family and dealing with a lot of things, but I will never again let a man tell me a lie or speak to me disrespectfully.

And I know all mothers think about their children first, but I'm here to say you matter as well, your feelings matter, and your mental health matters. And if you feel like you can't take it anymore, then DON'T.

Now I feel like my daughter is still my motivation and my strength and she is my whole happiness, and I just love to see her grow each and every day. But this I will say, you cannot be forced to be with someone you don't want to be with. Be wise with your decisions, as well and make sure he respects you and cares for you, because men love to fake it. I go through ups and downs and arguments now, but we learn to get through them as a family, and not having social media I can say made the relationship a little stronger. My daughter's smile is the most important thing for me in this world. And just let go and let God in and, eventually, we will be at peace, without arguing, assumptions, without family getting in the way, and just living happily ever after. Be patient, it takes time.

AMAYALYNN, AGE 16

My name is Amaya, and I am a teen mom. I am sixteen with a two-year-old daughter. Life was hard for me when I was a little girl. My mom was a single mom raising my sister and me. I did not have a father figure. Eventually my mom met my stepdad, and he filled those shoes in our house. I always knew my daughter's father. We grew up together because our families were close. I ended up getting pregnant because I was not open with my mom about sex, or boys, or anything really. I did everything behind her back. So, I tried sex with him because I felt comfortable, and I knew him, and I wanted to know what it was like. When I found out I was pregnant, I was so scared because I didn't know what my family would say or do to me. I ended up telling my mom, and we made an appointment right away. They were supportive because I was a good kid and into school and sports, and they still thought I could be successful. The hardest part of being a teen mom for me is worrying about my education, and I stress out a lot about how I am going to make it. The best part is watching my child grow up and learn new things and for me to learn new things with her as well. I do not have any regrets because I really feel that everything in life happens for a reason.

The advice that I would give other teen moms is to not feel ashamed all the time and don't let other people make you feel embarrassed to be a mom, because everything happens for a reason, and your baby is a blessing. I would also say to enjoy every moment because time goes by so fast, and they grow so fast.

Life is good right now for me. I am still finishing my education so that I can give my daughter and myself a good future. My daughter is two now. She is so friendly and so smart. She knows her full name, her age, her colors, numbers, and almost all of her ABCs. She also is learning manners and is already making me so proud of her.

SUZIE, AGE 17

My name is Suzie and I have an eight-month-old baby boy. Growing up my mom was a good mom. She was a teen mom too. She had my brother when she was fifteen and me when she was seventeen. She stayed with my dad until we were little, but he would hit her and do drugs, so she packed all our stuff and moved us out. She was a single mom for a while until she met a man she married and had another baby with. He was a really good father figure to me. I liked him. He was good to us, and my only father figure. He eventually got in trouble for illegal activities and was deported to Columbia. I never spoke to him again.

My mom was a good mom. She was really open, and when I started my period, she explained to me that I could get pregnant now. When I started having sex, I went to her, and she took me to the doctor and put me on birth control. I would get confused and forget to take it. I was fifteen and having sex with an eighteen-year-old and got pregnant. I think it was because I kept forgetting to take the pills. My family was supportive and helped me a lot and took me to the doctor. I found out that my son's father already had three kids from different women, so I left him, and I am raising my son on my own. I love my son so much and the best part of being a teen mom is the love, the cuddles and snuggles we get to share. I also feel that I am not alone anymore.

The hardest part is that I am alone when it comes to caring for my son, and it is hard sometimes. I will finish high school and go to college, because I want my son to have a better life than I had. The advice I would give to other teen moms would be to not give up and not quit. I feel like people judge teen moms so badly, and they are so mean to me. When that happens to you, try to stay positive and keep going for yourself and your little one.

JOHANNA, AGE 17

Dear teen moms,

My name is Johanna. I am a teen mom. I got pregnant at fifteen and gave birth at sixteen. My story started when I was five or six years old. I was abused by these older men that used to rent a room in my old house. They used to do stuff that was not even playing. It was a way to touch me, and they sexually abused me.

When I turned thirteen and fourteen, my life was nothing but bullying and abuse. When I met these people, I thought they were different. They seem like good people, but we don't know what's behind their faces. One day, they called me to go over and hang out, so we all went for a walk and climbed over a fence. Once we did, they drugged me with a pill and the little I remember is each taking turns to take advantage of me. When I would go to school, people would call me names like "Fish Lips" or hit me in a way like "playing," but in reality they just wanted to find a way to hit me. When I was fifteen, I met this guy. He told me he was eighteen, and since I was fifteen, I did not think much of it.

Fast forward to one time I went to hang out with him, and it was around two A.M., and he decided to go to the liquor store for a Gatorade. When I came back from getting his drink, the car was not turning on. So, he decided to call one of his friends to come and fix the car. He told me to go somewhere else while his friend came and fixed his car, so I did. I decided to leave and go down the street and take a left. I remember there were gaps between bushes, and I was hiding there. While I was there, I decided to call one of my friends to go pick me up so I could go home.

While I was waiting, he went to the street that I was in and got out of the car with a flashlight. He was looking for me in every bush until he could find me. He almost took five turns to look for me. I decided to go to the street because my friends were almost there to pick me up, so I tried to hide in front of a car. Once they came to pick me up, he saw me leave and blew up my phone with calls and texts.

After that I did not talk to him for a while. One day he texted me, saying, let's go out and go watch a movie at his house. I told him I did not want to and did not want to have sex with him. He continued and told me he promised we wouldn't have sex, so I went. Once we went to the room, he kissed me, and I could taste the alcohol. It was so gross. I asked him if he was drunk, and he said no, but I already knew he was. I pushed him away and said no, I wanted to get out, but he wouldn't let me.

I decided to sit down, and that's where he started. He pushed me back and got me by my arms and he got on top of me and proceeded to take advantage while I was trying to defend myself and get him off. I tried hitting him where it hurt the most. Nothing helped.

While he was doing that, he tried pulling down my pants, and I would try to pull them up, and he kept pulling them down he made it to the point I started crying. Once he was done, I wanted to run out and hug my mom.

After that, I found out I was pregnant. I felt something was wrong with my body. I decided to take a pregnancy test and that's when I knew my angel was coming along. I tried hiding my symptoms until my mom started noticing, and I knew I had to break it to her sooner or later. When it got to the point that I found out, I broke the news to my baby's dad. The first thing he told me was that it was not his and to make an appointment to abort my baby. My response was, "You're crazy and a psycho. I would never ever abort a baby, ever."

When I told my mom, she was mad, but she supported me. When I was two months pregnant, I had kidney stones. And I had surgery while pregnant. It was scary going through it alone. My mom was there when I woke up in the room. She was there for my appointment. As well as when my baby was born. When I wouldn't feel my baby, my mom would always make sure for me. She would lie down with me and feel him kick. My mom is everything to me. I am thankful for having an amazing mom and for her being an amazing grandma.

I stopped asking and worrying about my baby's dad in March 2021 when I was five months pregnant. When it came to his court date from his situation, the DNA test came out positive. There were so many problems with his sister. She tried killing my baby as well and would come at me every time and take advantage that I was pregnant and beat me up. Thank God I never came across her when I was further along. It's crazy how they can't even be there for my baby. It hurts, but it's okay because we have my family who loves us like crazy.

Up to this day, every text and everything that comes out of his mouth is a lie. I fell again and tried to make things right a long time ago, but he would lie, and up to this day he still lies even if I don't have contact with him. His girlfriend or baby momma showed me text messages where he would talk badly about me and my baby. It hurt for a time, but people like my family have love for us.

My story in my life still needs some accomplishments. It's not over yet for me. Soon I will have a high school diploma. And then my career. My advice to you is never to be scared or afraid to speak up. Always do what you have to do to make yourself happy and complete.

ABIGAIL, 17

My name is Abigail, and I am seventeen years old. I have a nine-month-old daughter. Growing up I was severely poor. Mainly because my dad would only buy beer and lottery tickets, I think. I would have to steal toilet paper from my school and take summer school just to eat. We lived in a two-bedroom house. My mom, dad, and little sister shared a room; they rented the second room to a guy from Mexico, and my brother and I slept in the living room. My parents only speak Spanish, and we don't speak Spanish, that is how little we interacted with them. In school I did well because it was the only thing I looked forward to. Around middle school my life started to get really hard. My dad would leave all the time because my mom was really abusive. She would make us lie for her to not get in trouble. He would take us on drug runs all the time and would attempt to drown me when I was not doing what he wanted me to do.

The man who rented the room in my house sexually abused me the whole time he lived with us. He would make comments about my little sister, and I was so scared that he would abuse her too, so I took the abuse, hoping he would not get to her. My older brother found out, and he was deported. He would write letters to my family telling them that I was lying and that he was not abusing me.

Before all of this happened, I had gotten student of the month every year. When the abuse started with my parents and their houseguest, I quit trying and I felt like I had no hope anymore. I gave up. The world was ugly to me. I was really depressed and wanted to die. I got in a relationship when I was twelve. He was fifteen, and it was toxic. He would put things in my drinks, and the police got involved. I had to give up my clothing for evidence because there was blood on my clothes. My mental health continued to get worse and worse. I started to lose control.

During summer school I met my son's dad, and at that time I was trying to heal from my childhood. I was really aware of what happened to me and how it had affected me and was trying to do better. I felt a little more confident. We started as friends and started hanging out a lot more, and it eventually turned into a dating relationship. The day after he graduated high school, I found out that I was pregnant. I didn't know how to feel. I just cried. I cried a lot. I started looking up what I should do and how to take care of myself and my baby. My pregnancy was really hard. I was really sick and lost so much weight. I could barely walk to school. I refused to stay home now because I was having a baby and there was no food at home. I would go to school with the same makeup as the day before, with throw up in my hair because I couldn't even brush my teeth or get dressed. Nobody knew at home, though; they never noticed. It was hard because there was dog poop all over the house. I spent a lot of time worried about my baby because I was so sick, and my home environment was so bad. CPS ended up taking us from my mom and so we went to live with my nana. My siblings eventually went back to live with my mom, but I couldn't do it. The smell of the house and the chaos really bothered me. I had severe anemia and would pass out all of the time. It was scary. I ended up having to go back to my mom's because my nana said I needed to go to foster care so she can get paid for me living there. I didn't have money to pay so I had to go back with my mom.

I was twenty-six weeks when I finally was able to get prenatal care. After I got the care, I told my family and friends. My friends all quit talking to me. My sister and I quit talking too. They would not talk to me. I felt really alone. My boyfriend would bring me a week of food at a time and drop it off so I could try and eat. My mom was so mean and would make me cry on a daily basis. When I got sick, she would say, "You got pregnant, what did you expect?" She would get on the phone and talk bad about me to her friends really loud so I could hear her.

I was cleaning my room all day, moving stuff and preparing for what I would do in case my mom kicked me out when I had the baby. During this time my water broke. I started crying and woke up my mom. She was having phone sex and didn't hear me come in. It was uncomfortable. She called my nana, and she took us to the hospital. It all happened really fast; I don't remember it all. I was uncomfortable because my mom was there. I told the nurses I didn't want her there, but they wouldn't listen. I would ask for a blanket and my mom would get mad that they did not bring her one too. She made it about her.

I was in labor for a little over a day and I had to have an emergency c-section. I was out of it. I didn't cry when I saw my daughter, I was in shock of everything that was happening. When I held her, though, I was so happy, and I loved her right away. She immediately started breastfeeding. In my head it didn't go how I wanted but I was still so happy.

My daughter's heart kept stopping so they rushed her out of the room. She had an infection and was admitted to NICU for four days. I thought it was my fault. I have never been so scared in my entire life. We were released and went home. When we got home my mom told me to get all of my stuff and leave. She didn't even say congratulations. She told me to get out, that I didn't love her and to go with my boyfriend. I called him and he came with his mom to get us, and we stopped at the weed dispensary for them on the way home but made it eventually. I felt relief to not live with my mom. The house was cleaner, and I felt safe.

I have been living here for nine months, and I am in school and doing better in life. I have started praying and going to church and I have more faith in God than I ever have. This helps me to be patient and understand that it was not my fault for the things that happened to me. Now I don't want to end my life anymore. I have a purpose. I am going to finish high school and go to college. I am motivated to make a better life for my daughter and to protect her from the things I experienced as a child. I still have hard days, but I love being a mom so much, and I love my daughter more than anything.

I have a lot of trauma from my childhood, and I am starting counseling and starting therapy and praying for healing, and I have faith that it will get better.

The best part of being a teen mom is the satisfaction of raising a kid I love so much and protecting her from the things in the world that I was not protected from. I also feel so much love for her, and I have never loved anyone like this.

Advice that I would give other teen moms would be to not let others take your joy and happiness. Just live life how you want, not how others tell you. Good luck!

ROSE, 17

My name is Rose and I am 17 years old with a 6 month old son. I currently live in a foster care home with my son. Growing up I lived with my mom and my dad. I had a rough childhood. My grandpa and my cousin would sexually abuse me and my mom was very abusive. She drank and did drugs every single day. She would throw things, break things, hit us and my dad too. I would hide under the table while she did it trying to hide. My older siblings were at school so I would hide under the table to be safe from her. She would use knives and wires and wooden spatulas to hit me. Wires were the most painful, I hated when she used those. They hurt and stung and cut through my skin worse than the knives did. Then one night when I was seven years old, my dad left the house in the family car to hang out with my uncle. I remember my mom was so mad and she was calling everyone to get a ride to where he was. She called my older sister and she came and picked up my mom and they went to where my dad was. She got the keys and got in the car and when she saw my dad, she pressed on the gas and re-peatedly ran him over. My brother jumped on the wind-shield, begging her to stop so she left. The police and ambulance came and cared for my brother who was hurt. He begged for them to check my dad, but they checked him first. The police came but everyone there was so drunk and so under the influence of drugs that they could not get a lot of information on what really happened. My dad died on the scene and my mom was arrested when they found her. She went to prison and two days later my sister came and picked us up two days later. She got custody of us but she was so much like my mom. She would hit us and throw things at us a lot just like my mom. I would steal food and money to get the things I needed like toilet paper and to be able to eat. If I got in trouble, she would get five of her textbooks and make me hold them on my head and stand against the wall until she told me I could stop. If I dropped them or touched the wall, I would have to start over again.

I began to have suicidal ideation. Eventually it got the best of me and I started to act on my thoughts. When I turned 15, I took a bunch of medine I found and stabbed myself in the stomach. I was sent to a mental hospital for two weeks. When I came home, my sister was so mad at me and yelled at me and said I was doing it for attention. I was home for two days and I drank bleach to try again. I stopped breathing and my sister dragged me to the front of the house where the neighbor came and started to perform CPR. I started having seizers and the ambulance came and took me back to the mental hospital. I loved it there. They were nice to me. They fed me, and did not hurt me. I did not want to come home and I was not ready, but I was released again to my sister. I would beg my family to take me back to the hospital. My sister told me that I was a spoiled, pathetic brat who deserved to be in a mental hospital because I told people what my grandpa was doing to me. She said you never tell on family and gave away all of my stuff as punishment. I drank a bunch of benedryl that I found to try and kill myself again. I was hospitalized for a month and a half this time. My sister called and told the staff at the hospital that she didn't care and did not want to take me back. I went to live with my aunt and was removed and placed in foster care. A social worker came and told me that I was in the foster system now, and that I would be living with my aunt. I begged the social worker not to make me go there. Her son was the cousin that sexually abused me as a child. Nobody listened and I was taken there anyway. So I ran away.

I showed up at a friend's house and their parents really stepped up and advocated for me. CPS agreed to move me. I went to live with another family in another city. I was not hit, but I did not get along very well with my new foster mom. I was told that I would become Catholic now and was to wear makeup and dresses to make myself more approachable to a men. I told her that I did not want to be Catholic but would consider looking into Christianity however. This was not an option. I rebelled against her and did not listen. I would wear sweats all the time and she would tell me I looked like a boy, or a lesbian and would make me do more chores. She started hitting my foster sister one day and she was only 12 years old. So my foster sister and I made a plan to run away. We saved all the money we could and finally got the courage and left. My foster sister went to her hometown and I messaged a boy I met online to ask for help. I got to my hometown and waited at a park. Some strangers were really nice to me. They bandaged my arm because I was hurt by my foster mom before I ran away. They also fed me and were nice to me. When they left I huddled up on a table and cried until about 3 am when I finally heard his voice. I felt so much relief to finally be safe.

His mom helped me again by standing up for me and getting me moved out of the foster home I was in. We started dating for about a week and I found out that I was pregnant. I was about two months pregnant when I told my new foster mom. She said she was mad at me, not because I was pregnant, but because she knew of the guy that was the dad and she said he was bad news.

I started walking to school and to doctors appointments and running away again. I ran away for two months this time without being caught. One day I was walking to a doctor appointment and saw my child's father driving down the road with a girl in the passenger seat. I flagged them down and asked for a ride. The girl told me that she was also his girlfriend so I broke up with him. He said that he did not believe me that I was pregnant so I invited him to a doctor appointment with me. He came and heard the heartbeat and we talked to the doctor. That day he quit answering my calls and texts after the appointment and I moved on by myself. I actually met someone else and started dating him. One day we were hanging out and my baby's dad pulled up with two people in the car. They all pulled guns on us and he said that

I was not allowed to be with anyone. They threatened me and the guy I was seeing and drove off. I was terrified so I called the police and reported it. He was pulled over and the police took the guns and arrested all of them. He left me alone after that and I broke up with the guy I was seeing.

My other aunt came to pick me up and my social worker came to tell me that I was going to live with her now. Her house was filthy, with roaches and holes in the floor and ceiling. When it rained, the water ran through the roof and would get us wet. She was a prostitute and the environment was so bad. She kept telling my social workers that she was working on it and they made me stay. I went in to labor and had my son. He was on time, but he was very small so he was placed in NICU for four days. I loved him already and was so happy to be a mom. My son and I left the hospital and went to my aunts again. My son's dad called when my son was 2 weeks old and asked to see him. I said yes, but he never showed up. It got really bad at my aunt's house too. She would try and give my son a bottle with soda, and would bring her clients to the house when she was prostituting. I never did have a follow up with my doctor after giving birth because I came home to chaos and couldn't get there. She was yelling at me one day and my social worker happened to call while she was yelling. He immediately came and picked me up. I was moved to my cousin's house. I am still living here. This is the safest place I have ever been in my whole life. They are helping me get a drivers license. They took me to the dentist. They don't abuse me and I feel safe here. I am not having panick attacks anymore either and I am in counseling to deal with the things that I have been through. I don't want to kill myself anymore, I have a little boy that I love more than anything and want to be here and be better for him. I am very close to graduating highschool and plan to go to college right after. I want to be an ultrasound technician. I am saving to get my own place so that I can have complete control over the environment that my son is being raised in and he won't have any of the bad experiences that I had growing up.

I love being a mom. I have never had someone love me like he does and I have never loved anyone like I love him. My son truly loves me. I have so much love for him now that instead of wanting to die to get away from it all, I want to make it better. I have a purpose that I did not have before. He is the most important part of my life and motivates me to keep going. Sometimes it can be hard because I am alone in life. It is literally him and me and that is it. When it gets hard, I don't have people to turn to or safe places to go for help. But my mental health is so much better and I have a reason to get better every day and to work on myself for him. My advice for other teen moms would be to not let the negative things win. There is ALWAYS something positive in every experience we have. Find it, and focus on that, not the negative. If I can do it, you can too!

Reminder

Remember that all moms feel insecure, all moms feel scared and have anxiety about their ability to raise a healthy happy child. As humans, we all get angry, scared, and make mistakes and have regrets. It is normal. Remember that you are worthy of a wonderful life that you will enjoy even more than the average person if you work for it and provide it for yourself while breaking barriers and accomplishing your dreams.

Being a teen mom is a hard thing. It is also a beautiful thing. It has the potential to destroy your life and the life of your child. It also has the potential to make you incredibly strong and so very successful. What it ends up being is up to you. And it starts today.

Lindsey Hoskins was born and raised in Tulare, California, and is now a teacher and a mother to three children. She works in a program for teen parents. She is passionate about her job, career, and family. She speaks Spanish and can crochet like any ninety-year-old woman. She was inspired to write a book for teen moms in hopes to provide a positive, uplifting resource for these struggling mothers because she has been there and knows what it is like. She was tired of seeing grown adults filming struggling mothers and getting paid to exploit their hardships. It is not okay, and she wants you to know that us teen moms are everywhere, and you can choose your own path. If you were a teen mom, and you would like to share your story for the next book, please email Lindsey at lindsey711@hotmail.com.

Acknowledgments

Thank you, Katrina S. @http://katrinaeditorial.com/, for all of your support and for pushing me to finish.

Thank you to all of the teen parents who were willing to share their stories to help other teen moms!

Made in the USA
Monee, IL
23 September 2024

66457958R00095